W9-BIC-550

Raintree Steck-Vaughn

Illustrated
SCIENCE
ENCYCLOPEDIA

Volume
14

MON – OHM

RAINTREE
STECK-VAUGHN
P U B L I S H E R S
The Steck-Vaughn Company

Austin, Texas

Copyright © 1997 Steck-Vaughn Company

Some drawn art copyright © Andromeda Oxford Ltd.
and Macdonald Young Books Ltd.
For photographic credits, see Volume 23.

All rights reserved. No part of the material protected by this
copyright may be reproduced in any form by any means,
electronic or mechanical, including photocopying, recording,
or by any information storage and retrieval system, without
permission in writing from the copyright owner. Requests for
permission to make copies of any part of the work should be
mailed to: Copyright Permissions, Steck-Vaughn Company,
P.O. Box 26015, Austin, Texas 78755.

Published by Raintree Steck-Vaughn Publishers, an imprint of
Steck-Vaughn Company.

Executive Editor   Diane Sharpe
Senior Editor   Anne Souby
Design Manager   Joyce Spicer

This edition edited and designed by Andromeda Oxford Ltd.

Andromeda Editorial and Design
Project Manager   Julia Roles
Editorial Manager   Jenny Fry
Design   TT Designs, T&S Truscott
Cover Design   John Barker

Library of Congress Cataloging-in-Publication Data
Raintree Steck-Vaughn illustrated science encyclopedia.
          p.   cm.
     Includes bibliographical references and index.
     Summary: A twenty-four volume set containing brief articles
on science topics.
     ISBN 0-8172-3943-X (set)
     ISBN 0-8172-3932-4 (Volume 14)
     1. Science—Encyclopedias, Juvenile.   [1. Science—
Encyclopedias.]   I. Raintree Steck-Vaughn Publishers.
Q121.R354   1997
503—dc20   96-11078
                                               CIP
                                                AC

Printed and Bound in the United States of America.
   3 4 5 6 7 8 9 10 IP 00

USING THE RAINTREE STECK-VAUGHN ILLUSTRATED SCIENCE ENCYCLOPEDIA

You are living in a world in which science, technology, and nature are very important. You see something about science almost every day. It might be on television, in the newspaper, in a book at school, or some other place. Often, you want more information about what you see.

The *Raintree Steck-Vaughn Illustrated Science Encyclopedia* will help you find what you want to know. It contains information on many science subjects. You may want to find out about computers, the environment, space exploration, biology, agriculture, or mathematics, for example. They are all in the *Raintree Steck-Vaughn Illustrated Science Encyclopedia.* There are many, many other subjects covered as well.

There are twenty-four volumes in the encyclopedia. The articles, which are called entries, are in alphabetical order through the first twenty-two volumes. On the spine of each volume, below the volume number, are some letters. The letters above the line are the first three letters of the first entry in that volume. The letters below the line are the first three letters of the last entry in that volume. In Volume 1, for example, you see that the first entry begins with **AAR** and that the last entry begins with **ANT**. Using the letters makes it easy to find the volume you need.

In Volume 23, there are three special features—reference charts and tables, a bibliography, and an index. In Volume 24, there are interesting projects that you can do on your own. The projects are fun to do, and they help you discover and understand important science principles. Many can give you ideas that can help you develop your own science fair projects.

Main Entries There are two kinds of main entries in the *Raintree Steck-Vaughn Illustrated Science Encyclopedia.* Many of the entries are major topics that are spread over several pages. The titles of these entries are shown at the top of the page in a yellow box. Other entries required less space to cover the topic fully. The titles of these main entries are printed in capital letters. They look like this: **ABALONE.** At the beginning of some entries, you will see a phonetic pronunciation of the entry title, such as (ăb′ ə lō′ nē).

In the front of each volume, there is a pronunciation key. Use it the same way you use your dictionary's pronunciation key.

Cross-References Within the main entries are cross-references referring to other entries in the encyclopedia. Within an entry, they look like this: (see MAMMAL). At the end of an entry, they look like this: *See also* HYENA. These cross-references tell you where to find other helpful information on the subject you are reading about.

Projects At the end of some entries, you will see this symbol: 🔬 PROJECT 1. It tells you which projects related to that entry are in Volume 24.

Illustrations There are thousands of photographs, drawings, graphs, diagrams, tables, and other illustrations in the *Raintree Steck-Vaughn Illustrated Science Encyclopedia.* They will help you better understand the entries you read. Captions describe the illustrations. Many of the illustrations also have labels that point out important parts.

Activities Some main entries include activities presented in a special box. These activities are short projects that give you a chance to work with science on your own.

Index In Volume 23, the index lists every main entry by volume and page number. Many subjects that are not main entries are also listed in the index, as well as the illustrations, projects, activities, and reference charts and tables.

Bibliography In Volume 23, there is also a bibliography for students. The books in this list are on a variety of topics and can supplement what you have learned in the *Raintree Steck-Vaughn Illustrated Science Encyclopedia.*

The *Raintree Steck-Vaughn Illustrated Science Encyclopedia* was designed especially for you, the student. It is a source of knowledge for the world of science, technology, and nature. Enjoy it!

PRONUNCIATION KEY

Each symbol has the same sound as the darker letters in the sample words.

ə	balloon, ago	îr	deer, pier	r	root, tire
ă	map, have	j	join, germ	s	so, press
ā	day, made	k	king, ask	sh	shoot, machine
âr	care, bear	l	let, cool	t	to, stand
ä	father, car	m	man, same	th	thin, death
b	ball, rib	n	no, turn	*th*	then, this
ch	choose, nature	ng	bring, long	ŭ	up, cut
d	did, add	ŏ	odd, pot	ûr	urge, hurt
ě	bell, get	ō	cone, know	v	view, give
ē	sweet, easy	ô	all, saw	w	wood, glowing
f	fan, soft	oi	boy, boil	y	yes, year
g	good, big	ou	now, loud	z	zero, raise
h	hurt, ahead	ŏŏ	good, took	zh	leisure, vision
ĭ	rip, ill	ōō	boot, noon	'	strong accent
ī	side, sky	p	part, scrap	ˊ	weak accent

GUIDE TO MEASUREMENT ABBREVIATIONS

All measurements in the *Raintree Steck-Vaughn Illustrated Science Encyclopedia* are given in both the customary system and the metric system [in brackets like these]. Following are the abbreviations used for various units of measure.

Customary Units of Measure

mi. = miles	cu. yd. = cubic yards
m.p.h. = miles per hour	cu. ft. = cubic feet
yd. = yards	cu. in. = cubic inches
ft. = feet	gal. = gallons
in. = inches	pt. = pints
sq. mi. = square miles	qt. = quarts
sq. yd. = square yards	lb. = pounds
sq. ft. = square feet	oz. = ounces
sq. in. = square inches	fl. oz. = fluid ounces
cu. mi. = cubic miles	°F = degrees Fahrenheit

Metric Units of Measure

km = kilometers	cu. km = cubic kilometers
kph = kilometers per hour	cu. m = cubic meters
m = meters	cu. cm = cubic centimeters
cm = centimeters	ml = milliliters
mm = millimeters	kg = kilograms
sq. km = square kilometers	g = grams
sq. m = square meters	mg = milligrams
sq. cm = square centimeters	°C = degrees Celsius

For information on how to convert customary measurements to metric measurements, see the Metric Conversions table in Volume 23.

MONOCOTYLEDON (mŏn´ ə kŏt´l ēd´n)

Monocotyledons form one of the two main groups of angiosperms, or flowering plants. The other group is the dicotyledons (see DICOTYLEDON). The forty thousand or so species of monocotyledons produce seeds containing only one seed leaf, called a cotyledon (see COTYLEDON). That is why these plants are called monocotyledons, or monocots.

The vascular tissue (xylem and phloem) of monocots is in scattered bundles in the stem (see PHLOEM; XYLEM). The flowers usually have structures (such as petals, sepals, stamens, and pistils) in multiples of three. The leaves are usually simple with parallel venation (see FLOWER; LEAF). There is no lateral meristem, so the stem never increases in thickness (see CAMBIUM; MERISTEM). Most monocotyledons are herbaceous plants. They usually have fibrous roots (see HERBACEOUS PLANT; ROOT). Some familiar monocotyledons are corn, grasses, cereal crops, and members of the lily, palm, iris, and orchid families. *See also* ANGIOSPERM; VASCULAR PLANT.

PROJECT 61, 72

MONOECIOUS

The larch, a cone-bearing tree, is monoecious—it has both female and male flowers on the same plant. Shown above is a female flower between two male flowers.

MONOECIOUS (mə nē´ shəs)

A monoecious plant is one that has both male flowers (staminate flowers) and female flowers (pistillate flowers) on the same plant (see FLOWER). These plants are different from dioecious plants, in which each individual plant has either staminate flowers or pistillate flowers but not both. Most conifers (cone-bearing plants) are monoecious, as are members of the beech, birch, and hazel families. Corn is also monoecious.   **PROJECT 62**

MONONUCLEOSIS (mŏn´ ō nōō´ klē ō´ sĭs)

Mononucleosis, also called infectious mononucleosis, is a disease caused by a virus (see VIRUS). The infection causes fever, sore throat, aching muscles, and swelling of the lymph nodes, particularly those nodes in the neck. The liver and the spleen

MONOCOTYLEDON

Plants such as grasses (above) are monocotyledons. When their seeds germinate, they produce only one seed leaf.

may also enlarge. Sometimes there is a rash. When the blood is examined, there are large numbers of white blood cells called lymphocytes (see BLOOD; LYMPHATIC SYSTEM). A person with the disease may feel sick for many months; however, recovery is usually complete.

See also DISEASE; INFECTION.

MONORAIL

A monorail is a train that runs above or below a single rail. Conventional trains run above two rails. The first monorail was built in Wuppertal, Germany, in 1901. It is still in use today (see RAILROAD).

Monorails have several advantages. Because they use only one rail, there is less friction. The reduced friction allows monorails to move faster and use less energy (see FRICTION). Monorails can be powered by electric motors, gas turbines, or gasoline engines (see ELECTRIC MOTOR; ENGINE; TURBINE). Perhaps the best-known monorails in the United States are at Disneyland in Anaheim, California, and in Seattle, Washington. However, some engineers feel that monorails are generally too expensive for use in conventional rapid transit systems. Nevertheless, monorails will probably continue to be built for special applications, such as providing transportation in places where there is not enough room for a normal two-track train.

See also LOCOMOTIVE.

MONORAIL

Monorail trains run on only one rail, either suspended below the rail or, as here, on top of it. This monorail is part of the mass-transit system in Seville, Spain.

MONOTREME

The platypus (above) is one of the monotremes, the most primitive group of mammals. Like reptiles, from which they and other mammals evolved, monotremes lay eggs. But like more advanced mammals, monotremes have hair, and the females nurse their young with milk.

MONOTREME (mŏn′ ə trēm′) Monotremes are a group of primitive mammals that, like reptiles, lay eggs. However, monotremes are true mammals—they have hair, and the females nurse their young with milk (see MAMMAL). The platypus and the echidna are the only monotremes that exist today (see ECHIDNA; PLATYPUS). Monotremes are restricted in their range to Australia and New Guinea.

Some biologists think that monotremes represent a distinct line of mammalian evolution, separate from the marsupials and placental mammals (see MARSUPIAL). The skeletal structures of some monotremes and their posture are more closely related to reptiles than to mammals.
See also REPTILE.

MONSOON Monsoons are winds that blow onshore during the summer and offshore during the winter. The best-known monsoons occur in the northern Indian Ocean.

Monsoons are caused by the unequal heating of land and sea. During the summer, the land is hotter than the sea. The hot continental air rises and is replaced by warm, moist air from the ocean. This moist air produces the heavy rain associated with summer monsoons.

During the winter, the oceans are warmer than the land. The warm ocean air rises and is replaced by cooler, dry continental air.

In the northern Indian Ocean area, monsoon winds generally blow onshore from April to October. They bring heavy rains to otherwise dry places. Monsoons occur on a smaller scale in Africa, Australia, China, Spain, and the United States.

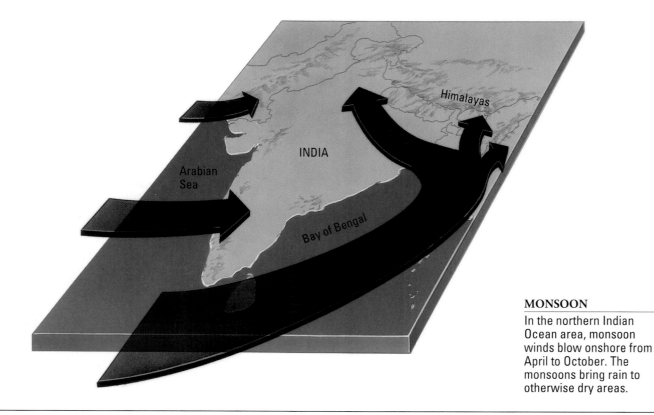

MONSOON

In the northern Indian Ocean area, monsoon winds blow onshore from April to October. The monsoons bring rain to otherwise dry areas.

MOON

The moon is a natural satellite of the earth. It is a barren, round body with no atmosphere, no water, and no life. The moon is the brightest object in the night sky. It is the only heavenly body to have been visited by people. The adjective *lunar* is used to refer to the moon.

Lunar statistics The moon has a diameter of about 2,160 mi. [3,476 km]. The moon rotates (spins) on its own axis (an imaginary line running through its center) as it revolves around the earth. It takes the moon 27.3 days to make one complete turn on its axis. It takes the moon the same amount of time to revolve once around the earth. The period of time it takes the moon to revolve around the earth is called the sidereal month. Because the moon's periods of rotation and revolution are the same, we always see one side of the moon. The other side always remains hidden from the earth.

The moon's surface gravity is about one-sixth of the earth's surface gravity (see GRAVITY). This means that a person who weighs 180 lb. [81 kg] on Earth would weigh about 30 lb. [13.5 kg] on the

moon. The gravity of the moon is too weak to hold an atmosphere around it. Since it lacks an atmosphere, the moon has great changes in temperature. The temperature during the lunar day may go beyond 212°F [100°C]. At night, the temperature goes down to -280°F [-173°C].

Lunar movement The moon follows an elliptical (oval-shaped) orbit (path) around the earth. The moon moves from west to east around the earth. From the earth, however, it seems to move from east to west. This is because the earth spins faster than the moon moves.

The moon's distance from the earth varies because of its elliptical orbit. The moon is closest to the earth at a point called the perigee. At the perigee, the moon is about 221,456 mi. [356,399 km] from the earth. At the farthest point, called the apogee, the moon is 252,711 mi. [406,699 km] from the earth.

The moon creates no light of its own. Instead, it reflects the sun's light. This light is visible from the earth in varying amounts during periods called phases. When the moon is between the sun and the earth, only the side of the moon facing the sun is lit. The unlit side faces the earth in a phase called the new moon. Under most conditions, the new moon is not visible in the night sky, because so little light reflects off its surface.

PHASES OF THE MOON

New moon occurs when the side of the moon facing the earth is not lit by light from the sun. As this side begins to be lit, we see a crescent moon (1 and 2). At first quarter (3) half the side facing the earth is lit. The lit shape changes to gibbous (4) before full moon (5). The sequence reverses and the moon again becomes gibbous (6), last quarter (7), and crescent (8).

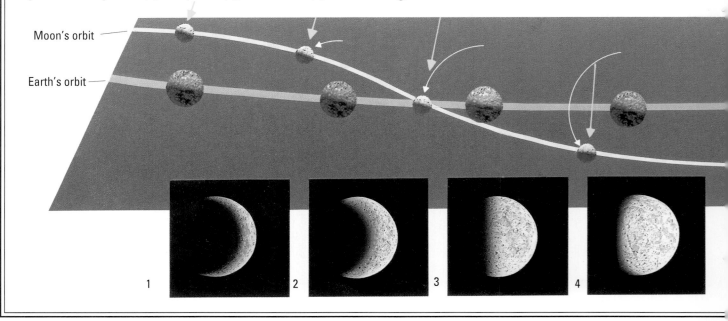

Moon's orbit

Earth's orbit

1   2   3   4

MOON CRATERS
The surface of the moon is covered with craters caused by colliding meteorites. There are also volcanic craters and large plains of solidified lava. These plains are called *maria* (Latin for "seas"). This photograph was taken during the Apollo 8 mission.

A little more of the moon becomes visible each day following the new moon phase. At first, a small slit of light appears at the moon's eastern edge. The apparent line between the dark side and the sunlit side of the moon is called the terminator. The terminator gradually moves west. After a week, half a lunar hemisphere is visible from Earth. This phase is called the first quarter. After another week, the earth is located between the sun and the moon. At this point, an entire lunar hemisphere is visible from the earth. This phase is called the full moon.

The moon is said to be *waxing* between the new moon phase and the full moon phase.

About seven days after the full moon, only half the moon is visible. This phase is called the last quarter. About one week after the last quarter, the moon returns to the new moon phase. The moon is said to be *waning* between the full moon phase and the new moon phase.

The time from one new moon to the next is called the synodic month. The synodic month lasts 29.5 days. Note that the synodic month is slightly

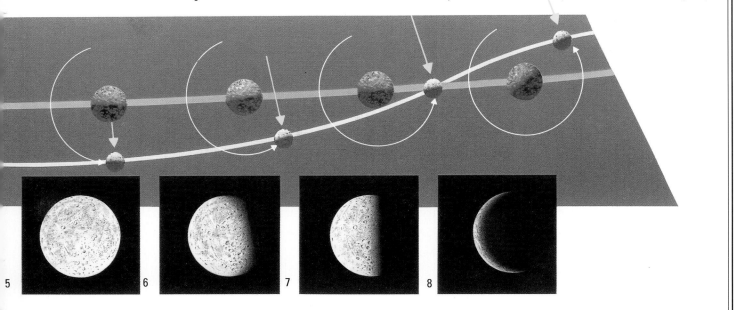

5 6 7 8

longer than the sidereal month. This is because the synodic month—the time between new moons—is determined by the relative positions of the sun, the earth, and the moon. These three bodies have to be in alignment for a new moon to occur. Since the earth is revolving around the sun, it moves along in its orbit over the course of the month. For this reason, to realign with the earth, the moon has to move slightly farther in its orbit around the earth. Thus, the synodic month is just over two days longer than the sidereal month.

Occasionally, the sun, the earth, and the moon will align in the same plane. Under these conditions, eclipses occur (see ECLIPSE). In a lunar eclipse, the moon is darkened by the earth's shadow. In a solar eclipse, the moon blocks the sun's rays from reaching a small area on the earth's surface.

The lunar surface The moon is covered with vast plains, high mountains, and deep craters (see CRATER). From Earth, the lunar plains look like dark patches. The plains are called *maria* (Latin for "seas"). The maria were filled billions of years ago by great lava flows from volcanoes on the moon (see LAVA; VOLCANO). The lunar mountains are called highlands. Some of the highlands are over 26,000 ft. [7,920 m] tall.

Craters are the most characteristic feature of the moon. Scientists think that there may be more than 500,000 craters on the moon that are each more than 1 mi. [1.6 km] wide. There are many billions of craters at least 1 ft. [30 cm] wide. The largest crater is about 700 mi. [1,100 km] wide.

The smaller craters may have been caused by meteoroids colliding with the lunar surface. Since there is no atmosphere to slow them down, the meteoroids hit the moon with full force (see METEOR).

The larger craters on the moon may have formed by collisions with asteroids (see ASTEROID). A few craters seem to be signs of past volcanic activity.

Valleys on the moon are called rilles. The straight rilles may be cracks in the moon's crust. The winding rilles were probably formed by lava flows.

Scientists have determined that the lunar soil is

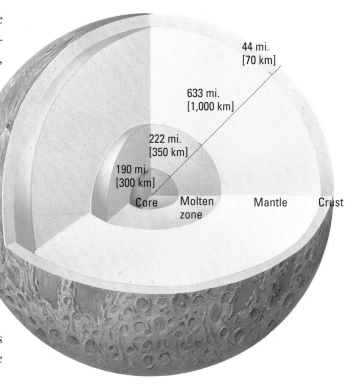

STRUCTURE OF THE MOON

The moon has a small core surrounded by a zone of partly molten rock. There is a thick solid mantle covered by a thin rocky crust.

made of rock and glass chunks. The soil on the maria is from 5 to 20 ft. [1.5 to 6 m] deep. No evidence of past or present life has been detected in the lunar soil (see EXOBIOLOGY).

The moon rocks are made of minerals consisting of aluminum, calcium, iron, magnesium, oxygen, silicon, and titanium. Two main types of moon rocks were brought back by astronauts who landed on the moon in the late 1960s and early 1970s. One type of moon rock is basalt. Basalt is hardened lava. The minerals that make up the basalt formed at temperatures of about 2,200°F [1,200°C]. The other type of moon rock is breccia. Breccia is composed of pieces of rock squeezed together.

Formation of the moon There are several theories that attempt to explain how the moon was formed. One theory says that the earth and the moon were once one planet. Eventually, the gravitational pull of the sun caused a huge bulge to stick out from the earth. The bulge separated from the earth and became the moon. Most astronomers do not consider this theory the most likely explanation. A more popular theory says that the moon was a separate planet that became trapped in orbit around the earth.

The third theory says that the earth and moon formed at the same time from gases and dust remaining from the sun's formation. According to the theory, the earth formed from the heavier elements, and the moon formed from the lighter ones. This theory seems the most likely to astronomers today.

Lunar exploration In the late 1950s and early 1960s, Soviet and American space probes transmitted photographs of the moon back to Earth. On July 20, 1969, the Apollo 11 astronaut Neil Armstrong became the first person to set foot on the moon (see ARMSTRONG, NEIL ALDEN). He was followed by Edwin "Buzz" Aldrin. Several other lunar explorations from the United States followed, during which many experiments were conducted (see APOLLO PROJECT). More than eight hundred pounds of moon rocks were collected during these Apollo missions. The data obtained has vastly increased our knowledge of the moon. For example, astronauts recorded magnetic readings much higher than predicted. This may mean that the moon has a liquid core, somewhat like the earth's core.

The astronauts left seismometers on the lunar surface to detect and measure "moonquakes" (see SEISMOLOGY). The seismometers determined that the moon vibrates like a ringing bell when hit by a meteoroid. This information suggests that the moon's interior is different from the earth's.

By international agreement, the moon may not be used for military reasons. This agreement allows the peaceful exploration and possible colonization of the earth's closest neighbor.

See also NASA; SPACE EXPLORATION.

APOLLO MISSIONS

Six Apollo missions landed men on the moon. This photograph shows Edwin "Buzz" Aldrin, one of the first to land on the moon from the Apollo 11 mission in July 1969.

MOOSE The moose is the largest member of the deer family (see DEER). It stands about 7.5 ft. [2.3 m] at the shoulder. Moose live in the northern regions of Europe and North America. They like to live in forestland containing swamps and lakes. They feed on water plants, grasses, and bark.

The moose has high shoulders that look like a hump. It also has a dewlap—a growth of skin covered with hair that hangs underneath the throat. The moose's dewlap is called the bell. The moose is brownish black on the upper parts, with gray or grayish brown hair covering the belly and gray to white hair on the lower parts of the legs.

The bull (male) moose has heavy, flattened antlers (see ANTLER). Each antler has short points, which stick out like fingers from the palm of a hand. The antlers are shed every year, and a new pair is grown. The antlers are full grown by late August and may weigh more than 100 lb. [45 kg]. The bull moose then strips off the dead skin ("velvet") on its antlers by rubbing the antlers against trees. A cow (female moose) has no antlers.

The mating season of the moose lasts from four to eight weeks in the fall. Baby moose are born about seven months later, usually in late May or June. A cow may have one calf, twins, or (very rarely) triplets.

Moose remain alone in summer. During winter, they tend to stay together in small bands. With their long legs, moose can walk easily in deep snow as they nibble on the twigs of trees. At one time, hunters killed nearly all the moose in the northeastern United States. In both the United States and Canada, moose are protected by law.

MORAINE

A moraine is an accumulation of soil and rock deposited by a glacier. This is a terminal moraine deposited by a glacier in New Zealand in 1750.

MORAINE (mə rān′) A moraine is an accumulation of rock and soil that is deposited by a glacier. There are different kinds of moraines. A lateral moraine is formed by rocks that fall into the crevice along the side of the glacier. A medial moraine forms when two valley glaciers combine and two lateral moraines merge.

A terminal moraine is a ridge of rock and soil that is deposited at the front of a melting glacier. Smaller moraines, called recessional moraines, are deposited at places where a glacier stops temporarily during its retreat. Such moraines often form ranges of low hills. Material that is deposited beneath a glacier as it melts is called a ground moraine.

See also GLACIATION; GLACIER.

MOOSE

The moose is the largest member of the deer family. It can reach 7.5 ft. [2.3 m] at the shoulder. The moose has high shoulders that look like a hump. Moose are most often found in forests that surround swamps and lakes.

MORGAN, THOMAS HUNT (1866–1945)

Thomas Morgan was an American biologist who was the first scientist to prove the existence of genes (see GENE; GENETICS). In 1908, Morgan began experimenting with a small fly called *Drosophila.* This insect has large chromosomes in its salivary glands. Morgan showed, in 1909, that these chromosomes contained the fly's genes. He was even able to show the position of certain genes on the chromosomes. For this work, Morgan won the 1933 Nobel Prize for medicine and physiology. *See also* CHROMOSOME.

MORNING GLORY

Morning glory is the name of climbing plants that belong to the bindweed family (Convolvulaceae). They live in moderate to warm climates throughout the world. The garden morning glory is one of the best-known plants in this group. Other members of the morning glory family include the jalap, moon-flower, scammony, and sweet potato.

The garden morning glory gets it name from the fact that its fragrant, funnel-shaped flowers open in the morning. They close later in the day when sunlight becomes stronger. The morning glory plant grows rapidly and twines around nearby objects. It grows from 10 to 20 ft. [3 to 6 m] high and is widely used as a covering for fences, posts, and porches. The garden morning glory has dark green heart-shaped leaves. The flowers are various shades of blue, purple, red, pink, and white.

Japanese varieties of morning glories have flowers that are 7 in. [18 cm] in diameter. The root of a Mexican species, called jalap, is the source of the laxative known as jalap (see LAXATIVE).

MORPHOLOGY

(môr fŏl′ ə jē) Morphology is the branch of biology that deals with the size, shape, and structure of living things. It includes the study of the external development of an organism, the relationships of its internal structures, and the similarities and differences among different races of the same organism.
See also BIOLOGY.

MORSE, SAMUEL FINLEY BREESE (1791–1872)

Samuel Morse was the inventor of the electric telegraph in the United States. He also invented a code for sending messages along a telegraph cable. It is called the Morse code (see MORSE CODE; TELEGRAPH).

MORNING GLORY

The garden morning glory gets its name from the fact that its funnel-shaped flowers open in the morning and then close later in the day. It is a climbing plant that grows rapidly. The flowers are shades of blue, purple, red, pink, and white.

SAMUEL MORSE

Samuel Morse was an artist, but is best remembered as the inventor of the electric telegraph.

Morse was born in Charlestown, Massachusetts, and studied painting in England when he was in his early twenties. He returned to the United States in 1815 and worked as an artist for a number of years.

In the late 1820s, Morse became interested in electromagnetism and its effects (see ELECTROMAGNETISM). Around 1832, he started to study electromagnetism, with the idea of the electric telegraph in the back of his mind. By 1835, he had made a working model of the telegraph, and in 1837, he demonstrated his first telegraph in New York City. In 1838, he developed the Morse code, a system of dots and dashes that can be used to send messages over the telegraph.

In 1840, the U.S. government granted Morse a patent for his invention. A patent is a document issued by a government. It grants a person exclusive rights to an invention for a period of time. Two years later, he supervised the laying of a cable at the bottom of New York harbor for another demonstration of the telegraph. The demonstration failed because the cable was cut by a ship's anchor. In 1843, the U.S. Congress appropriated money for building a telegraph line between Washington, D.C., and Baltimore, Maryland. On May 24, 1844, the first public telegraph message was sent from Washington. The telegraph made long-distance communication possible in a matter of seconds. Morse's invention began the communications revolution that is still going on today.

MORSE CODE

Morse code is a system of dots, dashes, and spaces that telegraphers in the United States and Canada once used to send messages. All letters of the English alphabet, plus numbers and other symbols, are represented by groups of dots and dashes. The Morse code is named for Samuel Morse, who patented his telegraph in 1840 (see MORSE, SAMUEL FINLEY BREESE). Several forms of Morse code were developed, including American and International Morse. International Morse is still used today.

The dot in Morse code is made by pressing down the telegraph key and releasing it quickly. This produces a rapid "click-clack" sound in the receiver at

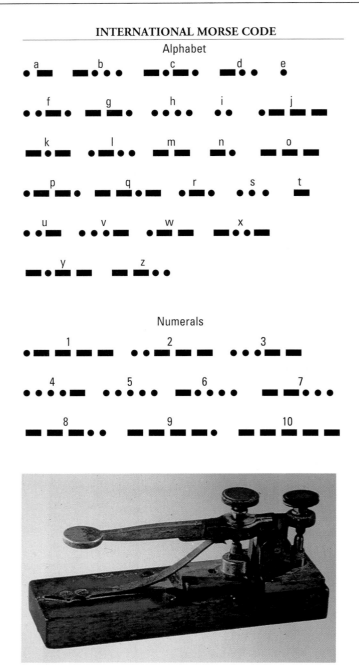

INTERNATIONAL MORSE CODE

MORSE CODE

Instruments called keys, such as the one above, were used by early telegraph operators to send messages in Morse code. A sample of the International Morse code, with its system of dots and dashes, is pictured above the key.

the other end. A short dash is twice as long as a dot. A long dash is equal to four dots. The space between letters equals three dots. A space that is part of a letter combination equals two dots.

MORTAR

Mortar is the material used in bricklaying for joining bricks together. The mortar holds the bricks in position and creates a tight wall. The mortar is applied in a pastelike form. It gradually

MORTAR

A worker called a mason uses mortar to bind bricks together. Mortar is a pastelike mixture of Portland cement, lime, sand, and water that will hold the bricks tightly in position.

dries—partly by chemical reaction and partly by evaporation—to form a firm bond between the bricks.

Mortar usually contains Portland cement for strength, lime for workability, and sand for economy and volume. Water is added to create the chemical reaction and to make the mixture easy to handle. The lime in the mixture reduces the chances of the mortar's cracking after it has dried.

MOSQUITO A mosquito is any of more than three thousand species of flies belonging to the family Culicidae (see FLY). Most mosquitoes have slender bodies that are 0.1 to 0.2 in. [3 to 6 mm] long and covered with tiny hairs and scales. The mosquito body is divided into three sections: head, thorax, and abdomen (see ABDOMEN; THORAX). The head has two huge, compound eyes; a long, tubelike proboscis; and two antennae. The antennae are threadlike on females but very heavy or bushy on males (see ANTENNAE; EYE AND VISION). The thorax has six jointed legs, each of which has a pair of claws. There are two wings that are very thin and almost transparent, with scaly wing veins.

Only the female mosquito is a bloodsucker. The beaklike proboscis of the female has six needlelike structures called stylets, which are used to pierce the skin of the victim. The female then squirts saliva into the wound to keep the blood from clotting as she sucks it. Most people are allergic to this saliva, and so it produces an itchy, red swelling. Some mosquitoes suck more than their own weight in blood from a victim. The blood is necessary for the proper development of the eggs in the female's body. Mosquitoes can get blood from all kinds of animals, including frogs, birds, and people, but each mosquito species has its preferred sources of blood. A male mosquito does not use its proboscis for sucking blood but for obtaining water and plant juices for nutrition.

Female mosquitoes attract mates with a high-pitched humming sound created by the beating of their wings. The wings may beat as much as a thousand times per second. The males pick up the sound with their bushy antennae.

After mating, the female lays as many as three hundred eggs either singly or in clusters called rafts. The eggs are laid in or near some type of water. Each species has its preferred place. A single female may lay more than three thousand eggs during her one-month lifetime. In warm weather, the eggs hatch into larvae in two or three days. These larvae are aquatic and are so active that they are often called wrigglers. Wrigglers feed on tiny organisms in the water. The wriggler molts four times in the next few days before becoming a pupa (see MOLTING; PUPA). The pupa is also aquatic and is called a tumbler because it tumbles around in the water. The pupa does not eat. Within four days, it develops into an adult (see METAMORPHOSIS).

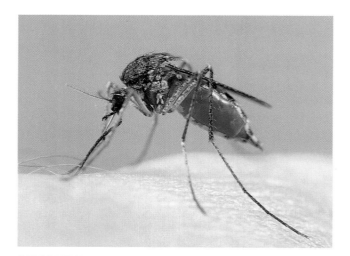

MOSQUITO

A female mosquito uses its beaklike proboscis to pierce a human's skin and suck blood.

There are three main genera (plural of *genus*) of mosquitoes that attack human beings: *Culex, Anopheles,* and *Aedes. Anopheles* transmits the disease malaria. *Aedes* carries the disease yellow fever (see MALARIA; YELLOW FEVER). Mosquitoes can be controlled by using insecticides or by eliminating breeding sites.

See also INSECT; INSECTICIDE.

MOSS, LIVERWORT, HORNWORT

(môs, lĭv′ ər wûrt′, hôrn′ wûrt′) Mosses, liverworts, and hornworts are small green plants that belong to division Bryophyta of the plant kingdom (see BRYOPHYTE). They are often called nonvascular plants because they lack the specialized conducting and supporting tissues (xylem and phloem) found in vascular plants (see VASCULAR PLANT). Most bryophytes have tiny stems and leaves. Although the bryophytes do not have true roots, they do have rootlike hairs called rhizoids. The rhizoids anchor the plant to the surface on which it grows and absorb water and minerals from the soil or the air.

MOSS, LIVERWORT, HORNWORT
A close-up picture of a moss (above) shows the spore-filled sporangia at the ends of long stalks. Small pointed caps covering the sporangia (below right) are shed when the spores are released. The male and female organs of liverworts (below left) develop on separate plants.

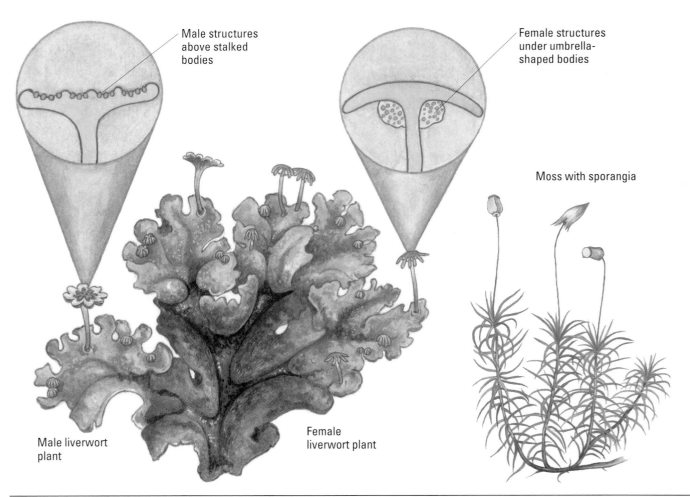

Male structures above stalked bodies

Female structures under umbrella-shaped bodies

Moss with sporangia

Male liverwort plant

Female liverwort plant

Some liverworts and hornworts, however, are seaweedlike plants, and have structures that allow them to live in an aquatic environment.

The bryophytes are very simple plants. For this reason, scientists hypothesize they may have been among the first land plants to have evolved (see EVOLUTION). Most mosses, liverworts, and hornworts grow in damp places, but some mosses can survive in hot, dry places.

All bryophytes have a sexual stage that alternates with an asexual stage (see ALTERNATION OF GENERATIONS). The gametophyte, or sexually reproductive stage, produces antheridia and archegonia. The antheridium is the male structure and produces flagellated antherozoids, or sperm (see ANTHERIDIUM; FLAGELLUM). The archegonium is the female structure and produces ova, or eggs, one at a time (see ARCHEGONIUM). When released, the sperm swim through the surface moisture of the plant to the archegonium. Inside the archegonium, a sperm fertilizes the egg. The fertilized egg then grows into the sporophyte generation, which reproduces asexually by means of spores (see SPORE).

The sporophyte is little more than a sporangium, or spore-filled capsule, on a stalk attached to the gametophyte. The moss sporangium has a protective cap, which falls when the spores are mature to reveal a ring of water-sensitive flaps. In dry weather, the flaps curl backward and allow the spores to scatter in the wind. In damp weather, the flaps stay closed, preventing the spores from getting wet. The tubelike sporangium of a hornwort splits open when the spores are mature and are ready to be released. The liverwort sporangium is a simple black sphere and, unlike the sporangia of mosses and hornworts, it contains no chlorophyll. When the spores mature, the capsule simply splits open to release them.

When the spores land on a moist surface, they swell and begin to grow. Moss spores produce a slender green thread called a protonema. The protonema branches and produces several new moss plants. As a result, moss usually forms clusters or cushions that increase in size as new protonemata grow from the bases of the old ones. Hornwort and liverwort spores do not produce protonemata

but grow directly into new plants.

Mosses are important colonizers. They are among the first plants to establish themselves on bare rock. By trapping dust particles and other debris, they help to form soil in which other plants can eventually take root.

Peat moss, or sphagnum, is moss that grows in layers over other layers of dead moss in bogs (see PEAT). In the United States, pioneers used to fill cracks in their log cabins with peat moss. In some countries, parents line their infants' cradles with the moss. This provides warmth, softness, and protection for the baby. In some countries, peat moss is mixed with reindeer hair and used to stuff mattresses. Peat moss is a main food of reindeer.
See also EPIPHYTE.

MOSS ANIMAL A moss animal is any of about 4,000 species of tiny, aquatic (water-living), invertebrate animals belonging to the phylum Bryozoa (see INVERTEBRATE). This phylum is sometimes called Ectoprocta or Polyzoa. Most moss animals live in groups called colonies on underwater objects in the oceans. There are, however, several freshwater species. Moss animals are so named because, in some species, their colonies look like moss.

An individual moss animal is called a zooid. Each zooid is about 0.04 in. [1 mm] long, though colonies may reach diameters of 40 in. [1 m] or more. Each zooid lives in a hard, chitinous case called a zooecium (see CHITIN). The zooid gathers food by means of ciliated tentacles—long, slender growths covered with hairlike cilia—that circle the mouth (see CILIUM). If disturbed, the zooid can retreat into the zooecium for protection.

Moss animals are hermaphrodites. They reproduce both sexually and asexually (see HERMAPHRODITE; REPRODUCTION). The larva settles on a surface and metamorphoses into a zooid (see LARVA; METAMORPHOSIS). The zooid then produces several asexual buds, each of which develops into another zooid (see BUDDING). The adult zooids are sessile, attaching to one surface for their entire lives. Some colonies contain millions of individuals.

Moss animals have relatively short lives. Death may be caused by the breakup of the zooid when it

Two small featherlike moss animals, called sea mats, are seen here growing on a piece of coral.

releases larvae. The shell-like containers left by the moss animals (and their ancestors—fifteen thousand extinct species) are the source of many of the limestone deposits in the seas (see LIMESTONE).

MOTION *Motion* is another word for movement. You are in motion if you are moving. Even when you are sitting quietly in a chair, you are in motion. You may not be moving relative to (compared to) the chair, but the earth and everything on it is moving around the sun. So you are in motion relative to the sun. In other words, the motion of an object is a relative quantity; it must always be related to another object. **PROJECT 32**

MOTION, LAWS OF English scientist Sir Isaac Newton proposed three laws that describe how objects move when forces act on them (see NEWTON, SIR ISAAC). These laws are called Newton's laws of motion.

The first law states that an object at rest stays at rest unless acted on by an external force. It also states that an object that is moving at constant speed in a particular direction will continue to do so unless acted on by an external force (such as friction, which slows it down). For example, an ice hockey puck will stay at rest until someone hits it. Once hit, it will move across the ice in a straight line at nearly constant speed. The puck slows down as other forces, such as wind resistance, push against it. This is also known as the inertia principle (see INERTIA).

The second law of motion states that when a force acts on an object, the object will speed up or slow down. A change in speed is called acceleration. According to Newton's second law, greater forces will produce bigger accelerations (see ACCELERATION). The law also states that a force acting upon an object will change the direction in which it is moving and that a more massive object is harder to accelerate than a less massive one. An example of Newton's second law of motion is when a person hits a pitched ball with a bat. Hitting the ball changes its direction, and the force acting on the ball speeds it up.

Newton's third law states that for every force (action) there is an equal and opposite force (reaction). When you sit in a chair, your weight is a downward force on the chair. However, the chair exerts an equal upward force (the reaction) on you. Without this reaction, pressure from your body would push the chair down. A spacecraft with a rocket engine is another example of this law. The force driving the exhaust gases backward from the engine (the action) is accompanied by an equal force (the reaction), which drives the spacecraft forward.

See also DYNAMICS; FORCE. **PROJECT 32, 46**

MOTION PICTURE

Motion pictures are a series of pictures projected onto a screen in quick succession to give the eye an impression of continuous movement. This impression occurs because of a phenomenon known as persistence of vision, in which the eye keeps the image—for a moment—of what it has seen. As a result, if the projected moving pictures follow each other fast enough, the eye will join them together to form a continuous image. Each separate picture, or frame, is slightly different from the previous one. Early cameras and projectors operated at sixteen frames per second. This caused a flickering effect, and objects seemed to be moving faster than normal. Today, films operate at twenty-four frames per second, which eliminates the flickering problems.

Cameras, film, and sound Motion picture cameras usually take pictures at the same speed as they are going to be projected. For slow-motion pictures, many more frames are shot each second. To speed up events on the film, such as showing the opening of a flower, one frame is shot every few seconds or even minutes.

Film for motion picture cameras is a flexible strip of plastic coated with chemicals that are sensitive to light. Both black-and-white and color film can be used in the standard motion picture camera. Motion picture film is made in several widths, which are expressed in millimeters. Film widths for movies shown in theaters are either 35 mm or 70 mm. Most film for use in schools is 16 mm. Most home movie film is 8 mm.

The sound track of a motion picture is contained in a narrow band along one edge of the film. Sometimes, in the case of special large-screen movies shown in theaters, the sound track is on a separate piece of film. The sound-track band varies in width and density. A light shining through the band produces a varying signal in a photoelectric cell in the projector (see PHOTOELECTRIC EFFECT). The electrical output of the cell is then amplified (strengthened) to produce the sound track of the movie. The sound track can also be contained in a magnetic strip that runs along the edge of the film. A magnetic sound track is of higher quality than the film type.

Animated films, often called cartoons, are made by using artwork instead of photography. Movements are created through sequences of individual drawings. Each individual drawing varies slightly from the preceding one. The drawings are done on a transparent material called a cel. The film is made frame by frame by photographing each cel against a stationary background. Some of today's animation is done by specially programmed computers.

MOTION PICTURE CAMERA

In a motion picture camera, unexposed film from the supply reel is fed onto the take-up reel. A mechanism stops the film briefly while an exposure is made. The star-shaped shutter rotates at the correct speed to make 24 exposures each second.

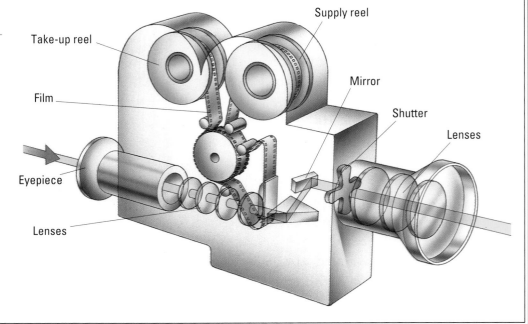

Take-up reel · Supply reel · Film · Mirror · Shutter · Lenses · Eyepiece · Lenses

History of motion pictures In the mid-1800s Hannibal W. Goodwin, an American clergyman, introduced a transparent celluloid film (see CELLULOID). Goodwin's film was tough and flexible and able to withstand the rigors of being wound on spools and run through cameras. Until that time, there had been no way to take pictures that could run quickly through a camera. The invention of such film was the first step in the development of motion pictures.

However, American inventor Thomas Alva Edison, or his assistant William K. L. Dickson, is generally credited with inventing motion pictures in 1889. Edison developed the kinetoscope, a wooden cabinet in which 50 ft. [15 m] of film revolved on spools. A person looked through a peephole to watch the pictures move (see EDISON, THOMAS ALVA).

Motion pictures were projected onto a screen for the first time in 1895, in Paris, France. A year later, in 1896, Edison introduced a projecting version of his kinetoscope. He held a public exhibition in New York City and showed scenes of a prize fight, a performance by a dancer, and waves rolling onto a beach. By 1900, motion pictures—or movies, as they came to be called—had become a popular entertainment in music halls and vaudeville theaters across the country. These early movies were silent. Dialogue was shown on the screen as printed matter, usually white type on a black background. The printed words interrupted the flow of action just long enough for the audience to read them. Sometimes, a pianist or organist in the theater played background music.

Hollywood, California, soon became the movie capital of the world. Several major studios were established there in the early 1920s, including Metro-Goldwyn-Mayer (MGM), Warner Brothers, Universal, and Fox. In 1927, Warner Brothers changed the industry almost overnight when it released the first motion picture with sound. The name of the movie was *The Jazz Singer*, and it starred the vaudeville star Al Jolson. Jolson sang a few songs and spoke a few lines of dialogue in the film. Soon after that, only talking pictures were made. The industry began to flourish, and it rapidly grew into an important part of the American way of life.

The usefulness of motion pictures goes beyond entertainment. Schools, businesses, and governments use film to instruct and inform. For example, many young people learn the basics of automobile driving without using a real car. A system of auto controls is linked to a film—or a computer-generated image—of road conditions. The would-be driver is given a sense of what it is like to be actually driving. Systems like this are called simulators, and they are also used to train pilots, astronauts, police officers, fire fighters, and others in professions in which training mistakes could be costly or dangerous (see SIMULATOR).

The beginning of television as a mass medium in the 1940s and 1950s seemed to be a major threat to the motion-picture industry. Many people thought that if free entertainment were available, people would not pay for admission to motion-picture theaters. However, in the long run, motion pictures have maintained their popularity. With the rise of video equipment, many people rent or buy movies on videotape and laser discs and show them at home on their television sets. Thus, motion pictures will probably remain a popular form of entertainment well into the future.

See also SOUND RECORDING; VIDEO RECORDING.

FILMING ON LOCATION

Scenes that are filmed outdoors, and not in the studio, are said to be shot on location. The location can be anywhere from a city street to desert or jungle. Location filming is sometimes difficult because the technicians cannot control the lighting or the weather.

MOTORCYCLE

A motorcycle is a form of two-wheeled transportation. The motorcycle works in a way very similar to an automobile. It has an internal combustion engine (see ENGINE). In an internal combustion engine, fuel is mixed with air in a cylinder. The fuel is ignited by a spark, and it burns. As it burns, it produces a large amount of hot gases. These gases push a piston along the cylinder. The pushing of the piston provides the power for the wheels.

Most motorcycles have between one and six cylinders. In an internal combustion engine, the cylinders have to be kept cool. In most automobiles, water is used as a coolant. In all but the largest motorcycles, air is used for cooling. The cylinders of motorcycles often have fins on the outside. This helps keep the cylinders cooler.

Like automobiles, motorcycles have a device called a clutch (see AUTOMOBILE; CLUTCH). The clutch is operated by a hand lever. It disconnects the engine from the gearbox. It is used when the rider is starting, stopping, or changing gears.

Most motorcycles have four, five, or six gears (see GEAR). Gear changing is done by the feet. A lever for the front brake is located next to the handlebars. The back brake is operated by a foot pedal.

PERSONAL TRANSPORTATION

Motorcycles (right) are a popular form of personal transportation. A motorcycle is cheaper to run than an automobile. Motorcycles of the future (below) will have an on-board computer. Called an embedded system, the computer will control fuel flow for maximum engine efficiency. It will also monitor the brakes and suspension.

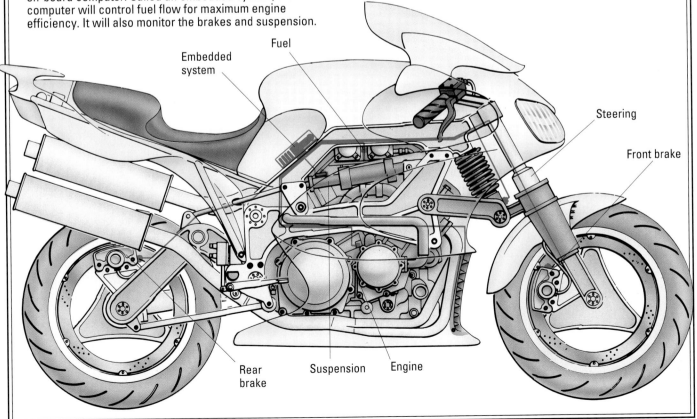

Embedded system · Fuel · Steering · Front brake · Rear brake · Suspension · Engine

MOUNTAIN

Mountains are landforms characterized by steep slopes, high peaks, and rugged terrain. Geologists generally agree that an altitude of at least 2,000 ft. [610 m] above sea level, or a projection of 1,000 ft. [300 m] above the surrounding land, is necessary for an area to be called mountainous.

Some important mountain ranges of the earth include the Rocky and Appalachian mountain ranges of North America, the Andes of South America, the Alps of Europe, and the Himalayas of Asia. The highest mountain peak on Earth is Mount Everest. This Himalayan peak is 29,028 ft. [8,848 m] above sea level.

Most mountains form by faulting, folding, or volcanic activity. Great blocks of rock may be lifted above the surrounding land because of vertical movements along faults. The mountains that result from this are called block mountains. The Sierra Nevada mountains in California were formed by faulting (see FAULT).

Some of the earth's greatest mountain ranges were formed by folding (see FOLDING).

High mountain ranges, such as the Alps and the Himalayas, may have formed by folding due to the sideways movements of plates (see PLATE TECTONICS). According to the continental drift theory, the plates that compose the earth's crust are constantly moving. When two plates collide, marine sediment is forced up between them. The Himalayas formed when the plate that carries India collided with the Asian mainland plate. The collision forced the Indian plate under the Asian plate, forcing up the sediment between the two plates. This theory also explains the discovery of marine fossils on the upper slopes of Mount Everest. The Appalachians

SNOW-CAPPED PEAK
Mount Rainier, in Washington (above), towers 14,410 ft. [4,400 m] above sea level. Conifer forests grow in the foothills, but nothing grows above the tree line.

Trench

Continental plate

Oceanic plate

BLOCK MOUNTAINS

The Black Mountains in Iran (right) are block mountains. They were formed when vertical earth movements along a fault lifted great blocks of rock above the surrounding plain. The blocks were then shaped by erosion.

Mountain range

Volcano

Molten rock

COASTAL RANGE

Along some coastlines, the continental plate carrying the land is over the oceanic plate (left). A deep trench forms where the plates overlap. Farther inland, the rock melts deep underground and forces its way to the surface. The chains of volcanoes that result become a range of mountains. The Andes Mountains, near the west coast of South America, were formed in this way.

may have formed in a similar way during an earlier time period (see CONTINENTAL DRIFT).

Volcanic mountains are made of hardened lava, ash, and other debris. This material is emitted from the earth during volcanic eruptions (see LAVA; VOLCANO). Most volcanic mountains are cone-shaped with a crater at the top. The Hawaiian Islands are a chain of volcanic mountains that have risen above the sea.

Volcanic mountains can form in a very short period of time. Paricutin is an inactive volcanic mountain in Mexico that stands 9,200 ft. [2,800 m] tall. It did not even exist before its eruption in 1943. In less than ten years, it rose 1,730 ft. [528 m] from its base.

MOUNTAIN ASH A mountain ash is a flowering tree or shrub that belongs to the genus *Sorbus* in the rose family (see ROSE FAMILY). Also known as rowan, mountain ash has large clusters of cream flowers and small orange berries. It is often planted on roadsides. It is not related to the ash trees, which are common in North America. Another tree, known as mountain ash, is a member of the genus *Eucalyptus* and is native to Australia. A specimen approximately 525 ft. [160 m] high is probably the world's tallest tree.

See also ASH; EUCALYPTUS.

MOUNTAIN ASH

The mountain ash is easy to recognize by its bright orange berries and fernlike leaves.

MOUSE Mouse is a name given to many small kinds of rodents (see RODENT). There are hundreds of types of mice. However, the word *mouse* is not the name of any one kind of animal or family of animals.

In general, a mouse is a small rodent with a body seldom exceeding 4 in. [10 cm] in length, not including the tail. All mice (like all rodents) have chisellike front teeth. These teeth are useful for gnawing. A rodent's front teeth grow throughout its life. Mice are found in all parts of the world. They live in fields, woodlands, swamps, deserts, and near streams. Most are active at night.

The house mouse is probably the most widely known type of mouse. It lives wherever people live. The house mouse often builds its nest in houses, garages, or barns. All house mice climb well. The body of a house mouse is about 2.5 to 4 in. [6.4 to 10 cm] in length, not including the tail. The fur of most house mice is grayish brown on the back and sides, with a yellowish white fur covering the underparts. House mice raised as pets or for use in laboratories may have pure white fur, be spotted, or be a combination of colors. House mice feed on any grain, vegetable, or meat they can find, along with items such as leather, paste, soap, glue, and paper.

A female house mouse may give birth every twenty or thirty days. She may give birth to from four to seven young at a time. Young mice stay near the nest for about three weeks after birth. Then they leave to build nests and start reproducing.

The American harvest mouse looks like a house mouse but is smaller and has more hair on its tail. Harvest mice build their nests in places where tall grass grows. The grasshopper mouse is about the same size as the house mouse. However, grasshopper mice look fatter and have stubby tails. These mice are so named because they eat grasshoppers. Grasshopper mice also eat other insects, worms,

MOUSE—Harvest mice

Harvest mice build a ball-shaped nest. It is woven out of dry grass and usually supported on large grass stems.

MOUSE—New and Old World

New World mice, from the Americas, include (1) the pygmy mouse of southern North America, (2) the deer mouse of central North America, and (3) the leaf-eared mouse of central South America. The Old World mice pictured here are (4) the harsh-furred mouse from Africa, (5) the pencil-tailed tree mouse, and (6) the spiny mouse.

and scorpions, as well as other grasshopper mice. The deer mouse is sometimes called a white-footed mouse. When excited, deer mice rapidly thump their feet on the ground, producing a noise like the rapid beats of a drum.

MOUTH The mouth of an animal is the opening through which it takes in food. In most vertebrates (animals with a backbone), the mouth is opened and closed by moving the jaws, although the lampreys and hagfish have no jaws (see HAGFISH; LAMPREY). The vertebrate mouth is surrounded by lips or a beak, and, except among the birds and some amphibians and reptiles, it usually contains a number of teeth. Lips, beaks, and teeth

may all help to capture or pick up food and break it up before it is swallowed (see TEETH). The mouth also contains the tongue (see TONGUE). Among the invertebrate animals, the mouth is a much simpler

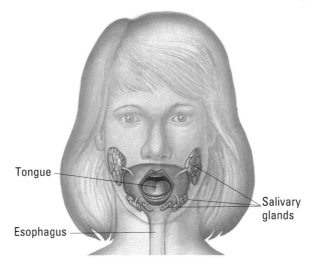

MOUTH

The human mouth plays an important part in digestion and speech. Salivary glands produce saliva to moisten food, which the tongue forces back to the throat to be swallowed. The tongue, lips, and teeth "shape" the sounds of speech.

structure. It may be surrounded by muscular lips, as in earthworms, but is often no more than a simple hole into which the animal pushes food. The invertebrate jaws, when present, are outside the mouth. They help to catch or gather food, and they often cut it up before passing it into the mouth. The mouths of many liquid-feeding insects have muscular pumps to draw in the liquid—often through jaws that are in the form of hollow needles.

MOVEMENT OF PLANTS One of the differences between plants and animals is that while most animals are able to move from one place to another under their own power, most plants stay in one place for their entire lives. However, some plants experience movements. For example, many plants produce mobile male gametes (sex cells), which swim about in order to fertilize eggs (female sex cells). Most other plant movement is confined to the movement of certain structures, while the plant itself stays fixed in one place.

There are three basic types of plant movement: tropisms, nutations, and nastic movements. A tropism is a directional growth response that is caused by a specific environmental stimulus. The direction of the growth is determined by the stimulus. A positive tropism is toward the stimulus. A negative tropism is away from the stimulus.

Tropisms are caused by growth hormones called auxins (see HORMONE). In most cases, the stimulus causes auxins to collect on one side of the affected part of the plant. This causes the cells on that side to grow and divide more quickly than the cells on the other side. As a result, the plant part bends away from the side with the most auxins.

Tropisms are named according to their stimuli. Phototropism is a growth response to the stimulus of light. In phototropism, auxins are concentrated on the side away from the light. This causes structures such as stems and leaves to grow toward the light. This concentration of auxins on the dark side may be due to the fact that light inhibits auxins on the lighted side. Roots are negatively phototropic and grow away from the light.

Geotropism is a growth response to the stimulus of gravity of the earth (see GRAVITY). Roots show

MOVEMENT OF PLANTS
Phototropism is the type of movement in plants that makes leaves and stems grow toward the light.

positive geotropism, while stems show negative geotropism. Hydrotropism is a growth response to the stimulus of water. Roots show positive hydrotropism and often grow great distances toward areas of moist soil. Chemotropism is a growth response to a chemical stimulus. Traumatropism is a growth response to the stimulus of an injury or wound. It often results in a bending or curving of the affected part. Thigmotropism is a growth response to touch or to a solid object. It can be best seen in vines and other plants whose tendrils coil around and grip any other stem that they touch (see CLIMBING PLANT; TENDRIL).

A nutation is a spiral growth pattern characteristic of the growing tips (roots, stems, flower stalks, and so on) of plants. It is a variation of tropic movements and is also caused by the changing distribution of auxins.

A nastic movement is sometimes called a turgor movement because it is caused by a change in the turgor pressure. Turgor pressure is the pressure of water in the cells of the plant. Photonasty is a turgor response to light. Thermonasty is a turgor response to temperature. These two nastic movements often interact in causing a response in a plant. The opening and closing of the stomata is an example of these two nastic movements (see STOMA). A plant's closing its flowers and "going to sleep" at night is another example and is sometimes called nyctinasty.

Thigmonasty is a turgor response to touch or contact with a solid object. The Venus's-flytrap, for example, shows thigmonasty when it captures an insect (see CARNIVOROUS PLANT). When an insect touches the sensitive hairs on the leaves forming the "trap," the leaves snap shut, trapping the insect. This response takes less than a second and is caused by a rapid change in turgor pressure. When a leaf of a sensitive plant is touched, all the leaves go limp and droop (see MIMOSA). This turgor response also takes less than a second, but the plant may need twenty minutes to recover and return to normal. PROJECT 67

MUCOUS MEMBRANE (myoo′ kəs měm′ brān′) A mucous membrane is a thin, delicate layer of tissue. Organs and body cavities that open to the outside of the body are lined with mucous membrane. Single-celled glands called goblet cells in the membrane make and pour out a thin, sticky fluid called mucus (see GLAND).

Mucus has many important uses in the body. Dust and microorganisms get stuck in the mucus that covers the inside of the nose and trachea (windpipe) (see MICROORGANISM). Tiny hairs, called cilia, gradually send the mucus and trapped particles to the outside. This stops the substances from reaching the delicate lungs. Mucus also makes the lining of the alimentary canal smooth and slippery, helping small lumps of food pass through the digestive system. The mucus also coats lumps of food, further helping the food slide along the alimentary canal. Mucous membranes also line the reproductive system, eyelids, and inner ear.

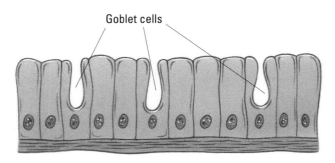

MUCOUS MEMBRANE
The cross section above illustrates the structure of the cells of mucous membrane, including the glands called goblet cells that make mucus.

MUD PUPPY A mud puppy is a large salamander that belongs to the family Proteidae. It lives in east-central North America. Mud puppies generally grow to lengths from 8 to 13 in. [20 to 33 cm]. Their bodies resemble those of tadpoles with legs. Mud puppies have large, red gills that stick out of their bodies just behind the head. These gills are used by the salamander to breathe (see GILLS). The gills of the mud puppy are like those of the larvae of other salamanders.

Mud puppies live in streams. They eat fish, crayfish, insects, mollusks, and the eggs of these aquatic animals. In some parts of the United States, mud puppies are called water dogs.
See also AMPHIBIAN; SALAMANDER.

MULBERRY A mulberry is a tree or shrub belonging to the family Moraceae. Mulberry trees grow as tall as 70 ft. [21 m]. There are four species of mulberry found in North America. The paper mulberry and the red mulberry are native to the continent, while the white mulberry and black mulberry have been introduced from Asia. Mulberry trees produce fruit known as mulberries. Although only the red and black mulberries are usually eaten by people, all of the berries are eaten by wildlife. Mulberry leaves are the main food of the cultivated silkworm.

MULBERRY
The mulberry tree bears edible fruits that look like blackberries. Its leaves are fed to cultivated silkworms.

MULCH Mulch is a layer of loose material that is spread on the ground around trees or other plants or on top of newly planted seeds. Mulch can be made of straw, leaves, tanbark (wood chips), manure, grass, or a combination of these. Mulch is helpful to gardeners and farmers. A layer of mulch helps protect the roots of a tree or other plant from cold or heat. Mulch helps keep weeds from growing. Mulch also helps hold water in the soil by slowing evaporation. As mulch decays, it turns to humus and enriches the soil.

See also HUMUS; SOIL.

MULE The mule is a hybrid animal that results from the mating of a female horse and a male donkey (see DONKEY; HORSE; HYBRID). A mule combines the features of its two parents. Like the

MULE

The mule is still used as a beast of burden in many countries. Here a farmer in southern Spain loads a mule with stalks of harvested sugar cane.

donkey, a mule has long ears, a short mane, and a tail with a tuft of long hairs at the end. Also like the donkey, a mule is sure-footed and has good endurance. From the horse, the mule gets a large, well-shaped body and strong muscles. Also like the horse, the mule easily gets used to a harness.

The offspring of a male horse and a female donkey is called a hinny. Hinnies are usually smaller than mules and are much less common. Mules do not have offspring of their own, except in extremely rare cases. All male mules and most females are sterile—that is, they cannot have offspring.

Mules resist diseases well. They remain strong even under harsh conditions. For this reason, people use mules to pull loads and do other work in construction camps, mines, and military zones and on farms.

MULLET A mullet is a saltwater fish that belongs to the family Mugilidae. There are six species of mullet in North America. Although they are saltwater fish, two species are also found in fresh water—usually at the mouths of coastal rivers. All but one species live in the Atlantic Ocean. The other species is found in the Pacific Ocean.

Mullets are heavy-bodied, silvery fish. They are about 1 to 3 ft. [30 to 90 cm] long. They eat some small invertebrates (animals without backbones) and also scrape algae from rocks and seaweeds. Some species also eat decaying matter lying on the seabed.

MULLET

The gray mullet, also known simply as mullet, is sometimes caught as food for people.

MULTIPLE SCLEROSIS (mŭl′ tə pəl sklə rō′ sĭs) Multiple sclerosis (MS) is a disease of the nervous system. It is believed to be an autoimmune disorder. This means that the body's immune system, which normally fights diseases, attacks the body itself. Multiple sclerosis is more common in cool climates (such as in parts of the U.S. and Canada) than closer to the equator. As a result, scientists believe that an environmental factor, such as a virus or a toxic substance, helps cause the disease. Scientists also believe that a person can inherit genes that make him or her vulnerable to multiple sclerosis, because people with family members who have the disease are more likely than others to develop it (see GENE; IMMUNE SYSTEM; NERVOUS SYSTEM). However, it is not known exactly what causes multiple sclerosis. No two people seem to be affected by the disease in exactly the same way.

Multiple sclerosis affects the central nervous system (the brain and spinal cord). Nerves that are affected lose their covering of myelin. This is a fatty material that helps them carry impulses, or messages (see NERVE CELL). Without myelin, the nerves can no longer carry impulses properly.

People with multiple sclerosis usually become weak and may not be able to move. Different parts of the central nervous system are affected at different times. Sometimes, parts that were affected seem to recover again. However, for some people, the disease gradually gets worse, and they become disabled. The disease is rarely fatal, however, and people with multiple sclerosis may live into old age.

Symptoms of multiple sclerosis commonly appear between the ages of twenty and forty. Even people who have been healthy all their lives may be affected. In about one-third of persons with MS, the first thing that is noticed is a temporary loss of sight in one eye. A complete recovery may occur, and the loss of sight may not happen again for months or years. Later, other parts of the central nervous system are damaged. The person has difficulty in walking, moving his or her arms, and controlling the bladder.

Considerable help can be given to persons with multiple sclerosis by means of special apparatus. Walking frames can help persons with MS move about by themselves. A number of drugs, including anti-inflammatory drugs and immune-suppressing drugs, can reduce the symptoms of multiple sclerosis.

In addition, a form of the drug interferon can slow the progression of the disease. This drug was first approved for use in the United States in 1993. Discovery of the cause of multiple sclerosis may lead to prevention of the disease.

MUMPS Mumps is a disease caused by a virus (see VIRUS). Mumps results in pain and swelling in the salivary glands. The main glands that are affected are called the parotid glands. Thus, the medical name for mumps is infectious, or epidemic, parotitis. The parotid glands are found in front of the ear and below the angle of the jaw. Therefore, mumps is characterized by swelling that makes the face look fat and distorted. Talking and chewing become difficult and painful. In fact, the name *mumps* is said to come from the mumbling noises made by infected people trying to talk.

Mumps is probably spread by tiny droplets of moisture that people emit when they talk, cough, or sneeze. The virus in the droplets settles in the mouth and nose of anyone who breathes them in. The virus enters the body and grows. It spreads through the whole body, not just to the salivary glands.

The signs of illness may not appear until 14 to 21 days after the virus first enters the body. The first symptom of the disease is usually a high temperature. The person may have a headache, a sore throat, and aching neck muscles. The salivary glands become tender and swollen. After about four days, the temperature returns to normal. After a week or ten days, the swelling of the glands disappears.

Very rarely, the disease affects other organs. For example, the testes in men and the ovaries in women may be affected (see REPRODUCTIVE SYSTEM). Very rarely, too, the membranes of the brain may become inflamed, resulting in the disease meningitis. In children, mumps is a mild, though painful disease. A person who has had mumps will usually never get mumps again—an example of acquired immunity (see IMMUNITY). Protection against the disease can also be obtained from vaccines.

See also DISEASE; INFECTION; VACCINATION.

MUSCLE

Muscles are the meaty animal tissues that contract and relax, allowing movement in the animal's body. Muscles contract and relax under stimulus from nerve cells attached to them. Many muscles are attached to bones. As a muscle contracts, it pulls on a bone to which it is attached. This moves the bone. In this way, muscles help animals move from place to place.

Humans have more than six hundred muscles in the body. Muscles make up about 40 percent of a person's body weight. Muscles do many important things. Muscles in our legs help us walk, run, and jump. Muscles in our arms help us write and hold things. Muscles in our chest let us breathe in and out. Powerful muscles in our heart work all the time, pumping blood throughout the body. Food is pushed through our digestive system by the action of muscles. Even the size of the pupil of the eye is controlled by muscles.

The different kinds of muscle There are three main kinds of muscle in the body: striated, smooth, and cardiac. Striated, or voluntary, muscle is usually under conscious control. Our arms and legs are moved by striated muscles. Most striated muscles are attached to bones and are sometimes called skeletal muscles. Striated muscles are made up of many fibers, each of which has small, dark stripes, or bands. Striated muscles can contract quickly and powerfully. They tire easily, however, and then must rest before contracting again.

A smooth, or involuntary, muscle is also made up of fibers. However, there are no stripes in these fibers. The fibers in smooth muscles are smaller than those in striated muscles. Smooth muscle usually takes a longer time to contract than does striated muscle. However, smooth muscle can stay contracted for a very long time because it does not tire easily. The walls of the stomach and intestines

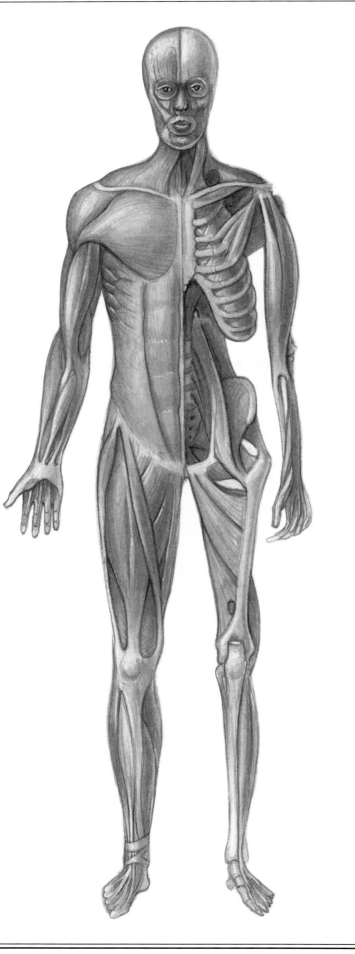

HUMAN MUSCLES

The diagram (right) shows the main superficial (near the surface) and deep-seated muscles of the human body. The skeletal muscles are attached to bones. When these muscles contract (shorten), the bones move.

are made up of smooth muscle. When this muscle contracts, it not only squeezes food through the stomach and intestines but also helps break up the food. There also are smooth muscles in the walls of blood vessels. These muscles squeeze blood through the blood vessels. Smooth muscles are not under conscious control. Instead, they are controlled automatically by the autonomic nervous system (see NERVOUS SYSTEM).

The third type of muscle, cardiac muscle, is found in the heart. Like striated muscle, it has fibers that can contract powerfully and rapidly. Like smooth muscle, it is controlled automatically and does not tire easily. Cardiac fibers are branched and interconnected. The fibers all work together so the heart beats powerfully and rhythmically (see HEART).

Sphincter muscles are special muscles that form rings around tubes inside an animal's body. They may be made of either voluntary or involuntary muscle. When a sphincter muscle contracts, it closes the tube. When it relaxes, the tube is opened. The pyloric sphincter, for example, controls the passage of food from the stomach into the small intestine.

Striated muscles and what they do Striated muscles are thick in the middle and thin at the ends. The fibers that make up the muscles vary in length from less than 0.04 in. [1 mm] to more than 0.2 in. [5 mm]. Each fiber is a single cell with many nuclei (see CELL). Many muscle fibers are packed together to form a single bundle. A single muscle contains many bundles. The muscle is covered with a tough material called connective tissue to hold all the bundles together. At both ends of the muscle, the connective tissue is stretched out to form a tendon. Tendons connect the muscles to the bones (see CONNECTIVE TISSUE; TENDON).

When a muscle contracts, it pulls one of the bones to which it is attached. The part of the muscle that is attached to an unmoving bone is called the origin. The part attached to the bone that moves is the insertion. Contraction of the muscle causes movements at joints, the connections between bones (see JOINT). The movement may include bending, turning, or twisting.

Muscles are not able to stretch. They can only contract and relax. Two of the muscles in the upper arm are the biceps and the triceps. When the biceps contracts, the arm bends at the elbow. The biceps,

ANIMAL MUSCLES

The cheetah has very strong muscles in the upper parts of its legs. Powerful contractions of these muscles send the animal rushing forward. The cheetah is the fastest of all land animals.

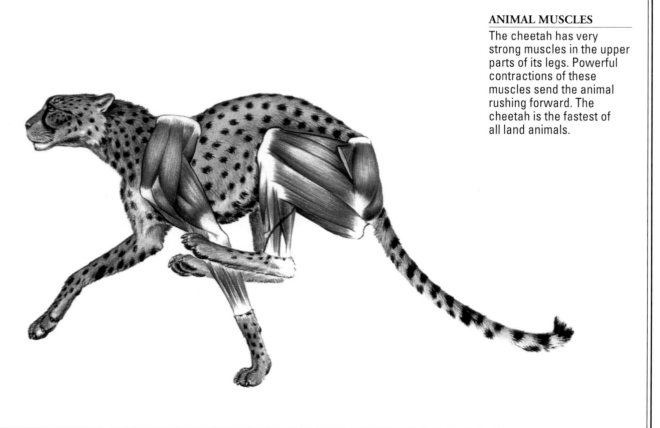

however, cannot stretch to straighten the arm. The triceps has to contract to straighten the arm, but it can do this only when the biceps relaxes. Muscles usually work in pairs. One muscle in the pair moves a bone. The other muscle in the pair returns the bone to its normal position. These pairs are called antagonistic muscles.

Muscle coordination

The movements that the body makes are smooth and steady. The movements are carefully controlled by the central nervous system. The instructions that make the muscles of the body work come from a part of the brain called the motor cortex, in the cerebrum. Another part of the brain, called the cerebellum, ensures that all the muscles work together smoothly. When you take a book down from a shelf, many muscles need to work together to carry out this simple action. The cerebellum gets all these muscles working at precisely the right time.

The brain must get continuous information about the position of every muscle in the body. It would not be able to control all the body's movements without this information. Nerve cells pick up signals from the muscles to send to the brain. These signals tell the brain exactly where each muscle is. They also let the brain know how much each muscle is contracting (see NERVE CELL;

PROPRIOCEPTION). The brain can then send out the proper instructions to the muscles.

How muscles work

The many tiny fibers that make up a muscle contract when they receive a signal from the brain. Muscle fibers work in an all-or-nothing fashion. They either contract completely or not at all. When only a few of its fibers contract, the muscle shows a weak contraction. The muscle contracts more powerfully when more of its fibers contract.

Laboratory experiments have helped show how muscles work. Tiny electrical wires were attached to a muscle. When an electric current was passed through a wire, the muscle contracted. This showed that the signals a muscle receives are very much like electricity.

The muscles in the human body, however, do not contract by electricity alone. The fibers contract in the presence of a chemical called acetylcholine. A nerve divides into many fine branches before it reaches a muscle. A signal from the brain travels along this nerve until it reaches these tiny nerve endings. As soon as a nerve ending receives a signal, it releases acetylcholine, which activates the muscle cells, causing the muscle fibers to contract.

Each muscle fiber is made up of many millions of tiny filaments, or threads. There are two kinds of filaments: short, thick filaments made of a protein called myosin and thinner filaments made of a protein called actin. The thick myosin filaments are sandwiched between the thin actin filaments. To contract a muscle, the actin filaments—pulled on by projections from the myosin filaments—slide between the myosin filaments. As the actin filaments slide, they pull the ends of the muscle toward its middle. A chemical called ATP gives the actin filaments the energy they need to slide (see ATP).

When a muscle contracts, it produces a waste product called lactic acid. If a person is exercising very hard, lactic acid may build up in the muscles. This causes the muscles to tire—a condition called muscle fatigue. Before the muscles can contract at full strength again, they must rest so that the lactic acid can be broken down and removed.

See also ANATOMY; LACTIC ACID; SKELETON.

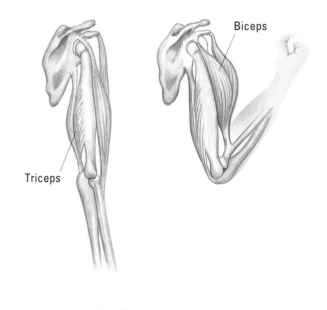

Biceps

Triceps

MUSCLE CONTRACTION

When the biceps contracts, it lifts the lower arm upward to bend it. When the triceps contracts, the arm straightens.

MUSCULAR DYSTROPHY (mŭs′ kyə lər dĭs′ trə fē) The term *muscular dystrophy* refers to a group of muscle diseases that are inherited. The cause of muscular dystrophy is a defective gene that is important to how a muscle functions. The defective gene may be either dominant or recessive. A person will develop the disease if he or she inherits a dominant gene from either parent. However, recessive genes must be inherited from both parents before a person will develop the disease. There is no known cure for muscular dystrophy (see GENE; GENETICS; HEREDITY).

The muscles of people with muscular dystrophy have certain characteristics that cause them to gradually deteriorate. Eventually, the muscle tissue is replaced by scar tissue and fat. The skeletal muscles, including those that help in breathing, are most often affected by muscular dystrophy. This makes it increasingly difficult for the person to move. The muscles of the heart can also be affected.

Duchenne's dystrophy is one type of muscular dystrophy. It is one of the most common muscle diseases in children. It affects only boys. Duchenne's dystrophy causes the muscles to weaken before the age of three. By the time boys with Duchenne's dystrophy are teenagers, they are unable to walk. Their bodies gradually become weaker, and most die of infection. People with Becker's muscular dystrophy, another type of muscle disease, usually live until their mid-forties.

Other types of muscular dystrophy usually do not shorten life expectancy.
See also MUSCLE.

MUSHROOM Mushrooms are fungi that bear their spores on complex structures called fruiting bodies (see FUNGUS; SPORE). Many grow in decaying vegetable matter and are commonly found sprouting from the layer of dead leaves on the forest floor.

Many people use the word *mushroom* only for a few species of edible fungi, and call the inedible or poisonous ones *toadstools*. However, scientists do not separate mushrooms and toadstools into two different groups. Instead, they consider them all, whether poisonous or not, as mushrooms.

There are more than 35,000 different kinds of mushrooms. The different kinds have many different shapes. Some look like umbrellas. Others look like a stack of shelves. Mushrooms come in many different colors, such as various shades of white, pink, lavender, yellow, orange, red, gray, and brown.

The mushroom grows underground as a mycelium. The mycelium looks like a web of threads, sometimes packed together like a mass of felt. The threads absorb food from the decaying matter in the soil. When conditions are right, the fruiting body is formed. In a typical mushroom, it consists of a cap and a stalk. The underside of the

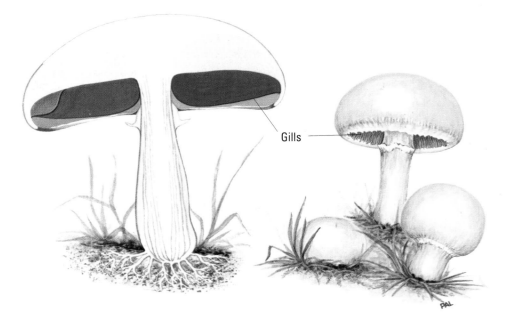

MUSHROOM

Mushrooms are commonly found in decaying vegetable matter where the mycelium of the fungus can grow. The round cap, or sporophore, pushes out of the ground on a stalk. Eventually, the underside of the sporophore breaks open to expose the gills.

Gills

cap breaks open and expands, revealing a number of thin growths that spread outward from the center of the cap. The growths are called gills, and they carry millions of spores on club-shaped basidia (see SPORE).

Edible mushrooms are grown on a large scale in darkened sheds with carefully controlled humidity, ventilation, and temperature. In most countries, mushrooms are considered a delicacy rather than a main food.

MUSKELLUNGE (mŭs′ kə lŭnj′)

A muskellunge is a large, freshwater fish that belongs to the pike family, Esocidae. It is found in a relatively small area from southern Canada to Tennessee. The muskellunge, also called the muskie, is one of the largest freshwater fishes. The largest reported muskie was 102 lb. [46 kg]. The present sport-fishing record for muskies is 69 lb. [31 kg] and 64.5 in. [163.8 cm] long. Its size and aggressiveness make the muskie a popular gamefish.

The muskellunge lives in weedy lakes and slow-moving rivers. It feeds almost exclusively on other fish. It has also been known to eat mice, squirrels, ducks, and just about anything else it can fit into its mouth.

See also PIKE.

MUSKELLUNGE

The muskellunge, commonly called the muskie, is a freshwater fish. It hunts mainly other fish among the weeds of the lakes and slow-moving rivers in which it lives.

MUSK-OX

The musk-ox has a large head, short neck, short legs, and a musky odor. Musk-oxen use their sharp, curved horns as a defense against wolves.

MUSK-OX

The musk-ox is a shaggy-haired animal of the family Bovidae. Musk-oxen live in northern Canada, Alaska, and Greenland, where winter temperatures fall to -58°F [-50°C]. A few musk-oxen have been introduced onto several islands off the coast of Alaska and also to Siberia and Norway.

The musk-ox has a large head, short neck, and short legs. It has a musky odor. Bull (male) musk-oxen stand about 5 ft. [1.5 m] at the shoulder. They weigh about 800 lb. [400 kg]. The cows (females) are smaller. In males, the sharply curved horns form a thick, bony plate across the forehead. Females and young have smaller horns. The musk-ox has a very thick, woolly undercoat to keep it warm. This undercoat is overlaid by long brown or black hairs, which reach down close to the ground like curtains on each side of the animal.

Musk-oxen feed on grass and low-growing plants. They are sometimes preyed on by arctic wolves. When attacked, musk-oxen form a circle with the young inside. The larger animals present a front of horns facing outward. Few wolves can get through such a defense. However, this method of defense does not work when musk-oxen are faced by human hunters, who can shoot them easily.

MUSKRAT The muskrat is a rodent found in many parts of North America and in parts of Europe (see RODENT). Muskrats are so called because of their strong, musklike odor. The animals live in swampy places near streams and rivers.

Muskrats spend a lot of time in the water. They have scaly, flattened tails by which they steer as they swim. The webbed toes on their hind feet also help them swim. Muskrats grow to about 1 ft. [30 cm] in length, not including their long tails.

Most muskrats make tunnels in the banks of streams. The animals live in these tunnels. Muskrats also live in "houses" they make by plastering plants together with mud. These houses often have entrances above and below water. Muskrats feed on green vegetation, berries, twigs, snails, and the meat from dead animals.

Female muskrats usually give birth to two or three litters each year. Each litter generally consists of three to eight young, although there may be eleven in some litters. As a result, the muskrat population increases rapidly. They can often overcrowd an area.

The muskrat has a coat of long, shiny hair. Muskrat fur, known as musquash, may be dyed to look like mink or sable and made into coats. Muskrat meat is sold as "marsh rabbit."

MUSKRAT
The muskrat builds a house made from a mound of twigs and branches. It also lives in tunnels dug into the banks of streams.

MUSSEL A mussel is a bivalve mollusk that lives in salt water or fresh water. It belongs to the phylum Mollusca (see BIVALVE; MOLLUSCA). Sea mussels belong to the family Mytilidae. Freshwater mussels are in the family Unionidae.

The mussel's body is covered with a protective shell made up of two pieces called valves. The valves are hinged at one side and can be opened and closed somewhat like a book. The mussel's body lies inside the shell. It consists of various organs, including the foot, gills, stomach, and heart. Like all bivalves, mussels filter tiny food particles from the water (see GILLS).

Several kinds of sea mussels can be eaten. The common blue mussel, which is from 3 to 6 in. [8 to 15 cm] long, is a popular food in Europe. Its shell is bluish black on the outside and pearly blue on the inside. Sea mussels spin tough threads that form a tuft called a byssus. The byssus anchors the mussel to a rock or other object, where it may stay for the rest of its life.

Sea mussels usually gather in large numbers, covering rocks, pier legs, and any other solid object. They can survive a high degree of pollution and are often found in and around estuaries and harbors (see ESTUARY).

Freshwater mussels live half-buried in the mud. They are a valuable source of shiny, rainbow-colored mother-of-pearl, which lines the inside of their shells. Mother-of-pearl is used to make buttons and other objects.

MUSSEL
Mussels, such as the sea species above, are bivalve mollusks. They are called bivalves because they have two-piece shells. Some mussels are eaten by people.

MUSTARD FAMILY The mustard family (Cruciferae or Brassicaceae) includes about 3,200 species of plants, most of which are herbaceous species native to temperate areas of the world. They are dicotyledons, and their flowers have four sepals and four petals arranged in a cross. The flowers are mainly white or yellow. There are six stamens, two of which are usually shorter than the others (see DICOTYLEDON; FLOWER; HERBACEOUS PLANT).

One of the most important genera of the mustard family is *Brassica*. Members of this genus include the cabbages in all their varieties—such as cauliflower, broccoli, and Brussels sprouts—turnips, swedes, and some of the mustards. Mustard seeds contain a pungent oil that is used as a spice, in medicines, and in mustard plasters used for pain relief. Seeds of the European black mustard were once the main source of commercial mustard products, but they have now been replaced in most areas by brown mustard, which originated in Africa or Asia. The European white mustard is still cultivated on a large scale in the United States and is the basis of most American mustard products. Other members of the mustard family include horseradish and wallflowers.

MUSTARD FAMILY

Today black mustard is grown mainly for soil cover or grazing. It has bright yellow flowers.

MUTATION A mutation is a change in an inherited characteristic that is caused by a change in one or more genes (see GENE). As the result of a mutation, an offspring inherits a characteristic that was not present in either of the parents. This new characteristic is part of the offspring's genetic code and will be passed on to future generations (see HEREDITY).

An organism that has undergone a mutation is called a mutant. Most mutations are harmful to the organism, often causing its death before the organism is able to reproduce and pass on the mutated gene. Some mutations, however, are helpful. Mutations are an important part of the process of evolution (see EVOLUTION; VARIATION).

A mutation is either spontaneous or induced. A spontaneous mutation is a change in the structure of DNA in a gene that occurs during mitosis, meiosis, or any other normal cell process (see DNA;

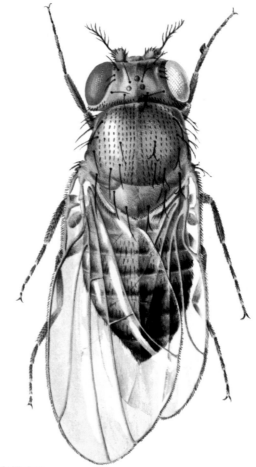

MUTATION

Drosophila melanogaster, a kind of fruit fly, is shown (above). Normally, these flies have red eyes and large wings. The white eye and small wing on the right side are mutations.

MEIOSIS; MITOSIS). An induced mutation is externally caused by such factors as drugs, X rays, or other types of radiation.

See also GENETICS.

MYNA

The Indian myna is related to the starling. A native of India, it has now spread to Australia and islands of the Indian Ocean.

MYNA (mī′ nə) *Myna* is the name given to several types of birds in the starling family. Myna birds are native to India, and other parts of Asia. These birds are usually quite social. They often build nests in cracks and various other parts of buildings. Myna birds are sometimes seen perched on the backs of cattle. They feed on insects, worms, and fruit.

The common house myna is slightly larger than the American robin. The house myna has attractive coloring, ranging from reddish brown on the lower breast to deep black on the upper breast, neck, and head. The house myna's bill and legs are a bright yellow. The crested myna lives in cultivated fields and pastures. This bird is often found in highly populated areas. The talking myna is often kept as a pet because it can mimic a wide variety of sounds, rather like a parrot. The myna has been introduced in North America, though its range has not spread far.

MYRTLE FAMILY The myrtle (mûr′tl) family, Myrtaceae, includes about three thousand species of evergreen trees and shrubs that grow in tropical and subtropical regions. They have simple, opposite leaves that often contain strongly scented oils (see EVERGREEN; LEAF). Their flowers are often large and elaborate with four or five overlapping sepals, four or five petals, and many stamens (see FLOWER).

Members of the myrtle family include the bayberry, clove, and eucalyptus. The myrtles (genus *Myrtus*) include about one hundred species, some of which produce edible berries. The leaves of the common myrtle are used to make perfume.

See also EUCALYPTUS.

MYRTLE FAMILY

The common myrtle, pictured here, grows in southern Europe and western Asia. It has blue-black berries and aromatic evergreen leaves. The leaves are used to make perfume.

N

NADIR (nā′ dər) The nadir is the point on the celestial sphere directly below an observer. The opposite of the nadir is the zenith.
See also CELESTIAL SPHERE; ZENITH.

NAIL Nails are hard, flattened growths from the fingers and toes of human beings, apes, and many monkeys. Most other mammals have sharp claws, and so do birds and many reptiles. Horses and cattle and their relatives have blunt hooves. All these growths are formed from the outer layer of the skin, the epidermis (see SKIN). The growths consist of hardened skin cells, which contain a material called keratin (see KERATIN).

The skin below the nail is called the nail matrix. Near the root of the nail, the cells of this skin are smaller. They carry less blood. The white, circular spot containing these cells is called the lunula. If a nail is torn off, it will grow again as long as the matrix has not been severely injured. The state of a person's health is often indicated by his or her nails. Illness can affect their growth.

NAPHTHALENE (năf′ thə lēn′) Naphthalene ($C_{10}H_8$) is a white crystalline solid. A molecule of naphthalene consists of two benzene molecules joined together along one side (see BENZENE; CRYSTAL). Most naphthalene is used to make dyes and plastics. The smell of naphthalene repels insects and is used to keep clothes free of moths. Naphthalene is also used in pesticides. It helps keep soil and plants free of pests.
See also PESTICIDE.

NARCISSUS (när sĭs′ əs) Narcissus is a genus of about sixty species of flowering plants belonging to the amaryllis family (see AMARYLLIS FAMILY). They are native to Europe and Asia and are cultivated worldwide for their beautiful, fragrant flowers. They grow from poisonous brown bulbs (see BULB AND CORM). A single white, yellow, or pink flower grows at the end of a tall stalk, which rises above the sword-shaped leaves. The flower has six petals surrounding a trumpet-shaped tube called the corona. Two popular wild species are the daffodil and the poet's narcissus. These have been cultivated for a long time, and many different forms and hybrids now exist in gardens.

The name *narcissus* comes from Greek mythology. According to the myth, Narcissus was the son of a god. He was so selfish and so overly concerned with his good looks that the other gods decided to punish him. They made him fall in love with his own reflection in a pond. Narcissus was so in love that he refused to leave his reflection for even a minute. When he died, the gods turned him into a flower—the narcissus.

NARCISSUS

The narcissus, like the closely related daffodil, is a popular garden flower in the spring.

NARCOTIC (när kŏt′ ĭk) Scientists define narcotics as those drugs that are strong depressants. Depressants slow the activities of the nervous system (see NERVOUS SYSTEM). Other effects of narcotics vary from user to user. However, most narcotics users experience drowsiness and a false sense of well-being and contentment, often called a "high." Narcotics such as heroin, morphine, and opium are obtained from the opium poppy. Narcotics can also be synthetic (human-made). Methadone is an example of a synthetic narcotic (see DRUG; POPPY FAMILY).

When narcotics depress the nervous system, they suppress the ability of nerves to pass along pain impulses. These pain impulses, then, are not perceived by the brain. For this reason, narcotics have been used for thousands of years to relieve pain. The ancient Greeks and Romans began using opium to relieve pain about six thousand years ago. The Chinese began using opium to relieve pain about A.D. 600. Later, they used opium for the "high" it produced. In the mid-1800s, doctors and others in the United States began to use morphine and heroin to relieve pain. Morphine is made from opium and is stronger than opium. Heroin is made from morphine and is stronger than morphine. Nonmedical use of narcotics became illegal in the United States when Congress passed the Harrison Narcotics Act in 1915. In spite of the act, the illegal use of morphine and heroin became widespread in the 1960s and 1970s.

The effects of narcotics may last from three to six hours, depending on the user and the kind and amount of narcotics used. Narcotics are addictive drugs (see ADDICTION). Users also may develop a tolerance to narcotics. This means that they have to take increasing amounts of the drugs to achieve the same effects. As the effects wear off, users may experience cramps, nausea, and extreme restlessness. These symptoms force the user to seek another dose of narcotics. The use of narcotics often interferes with an individual's ability to hold a job. Users then often steal or do other illegal acts to get money for narcotics. Narcotics use has other effects, depending on the individual. For example, some addicts become withdrawn or irritable and unwilling or unable to maintain normal social contacts.

Those who are addicted to narcotics may receive help from professional treatment programs. Some treatment programs rely on psychological therapy (see PSYCHOLOGY). Therapy also tries to help addicts understand the causes of their drug use. Therapy also helps the addict change so that he or she can live a drug-free life. Before therapy begins, the addict may undergo detoxification. During detoxification, the addict stops using narcotics and tries to rid his or her body of them.

Other experimental treatment programs are based on "drug maintenance." Drug maintenance programs relieve the physical cravings for narcotics by giving the addict small doses of a legal narcotic, such as methadone. This helps keep the addict from stealing or performing other illegal acts to get money for illegal narcotics. Many drug maintenance programs also provide psychological therapy. Drug maintenance programs are controversial because addicts may have to take methadone for the rest of their lives.

NARWHAL (när' wəl) The narwhal is a grayish white, dark-spotted whale found in the Arctic Ocean. The male is noted for its spiral tusk, which is about 8 ft. [2.4 m] in length. This tusk sticks out of the left side of the male's head. The tusk is the narwhal's only tooth. Females usually do not have tusks. However, when they do have tusks, they almost always have two of them. Male narwhals fight with their tusks during the breeding season.

Narwhals grow about 18 ft. [5.5 m] in length, not including the tusk. The animals may weigh up to 2 tons [1.8 metric tons]. Narwhals feed mainly on soft squids and cuttlefish. Some Eskimos hunt these whales. The skin and flesh are eaten. The tusks are made into tools and ornaments.
See also WHALE.

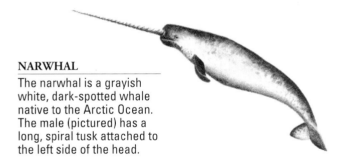

NARWHAL
The narwhal is a grayish white, dark-spotted whale native to the Arctic Ocean. The male (pictured) has a long, spiral tusk attached to the left side of the head.

NASA The National Aeronautics and Space Administration, or NASA, is the government agency that runs the United States space program. NASA was established in 1958 and is headquartered in Washington, D.C.

The John F. Kennedy Space Center at Cape Canaveral, Florida, is where most spacecraft are launched. The Lyndon B. Johnson Space Center in Houston, Texas, is the control center for manned space flights. Satellites and space probes are monitored from the Goddard Space Flight Center in Greenbelt, Maryland. NASA operates several other research and development facilities in various parts of the country.

See also CAPE CANAVERAL; SPACE EXPLORATION.

NASTURTIUM (nə stûr′ shəm)

Nasturtium is the name given to plants of the genus *Tropaeolum*. They are native to tropical areas in the Americas. Common nasturtium is a scrambling or climbing plant that grows to a length of about 10 ft. [3 m]. Its flowers are yellow, orange, or red. Each flower has five sepals. Three of the sepals form a nectar-containing tube called a spur. Nectar is a sweet liquid secreted by some plants. There are also five petals. The leaves have a peppery taste and are sometimes used in salads.

See also CLIMBING PLANT; FLOWER.

NASTURTIUM

Nasturtiums are colorful plants native to tropical areas of the Americas. The leaves of nasturtiums are sometimes eaten in salads, and the seeds may be pickled.

NATIONAL PARK

A national park is land that has been acquired by the federal government of the United States for the purpose of recreation and conserving wildlife, natural resources, and beautiful scenery (see CONSERVATION; NATURAL RESOURCE). The first national park in the United States, Yellowstone National Park, was created in 1872. Yellowstone, located in Wyoming, was founded in order to protect many species of animals that were becoming rare. Today, Yellowstone has more grizzly bears than most places in the lower

NATIONAL PARK

Glacier Bay National Park in Alaska is famous for its rocky peaks and lakes formed by water from melted ice and snow.

United States (see GRIZZLY BEAR). The park also has springs of boiling water, geysers that shoot water high into the air, and beautiful waterfalls (see SPRING AND GEYSER; WATERFALL AND RAPID). If the park had not been established, the bears might have been killed off as they were in other areas, the springs drained, and the waterfalls dammed. Yellowstone National Park, like other national parks, makes sure that these natural wonders are protected for everyone to enjoy for many years to come.

National parks in the United States now occupy more than 79 million acres [32 million hectares] of land, an area larger than Missouri and Iowa combined. The parks include deserts, forests, mountains, prairies, rivers, and seashores. Many species of plants and animals are protected in these parks. The idea of national parks has spread to other places too. There are now more than 3,500 national parks and wildlife reserves around the world. For example, Africa has huge parks where antelopes, baboons, elephants, giraffes, and lions roam freely.

Scientists often use national parks to study plants and animals in a natural setting. Every year, thousands of people visit and camp in national parks. Restaurants, motels, and gas stations are built to serve the thousands of visitors.

Many states in the United States now have state parks. These parks are similar to the national parks except that they are owned and operated by the state governments instead of the federal government.

NATURAL GAS Natural gas is a chemical in gaseous form that is made of hydrocarbons. Hydrocarbons are compounds that contain carbon and hydrogen. Natural gas is mainly made of one type of hydrocarbon, methane. Natural gas is often used as fuel. Natural gas, often called gas, should not be confused with gasoline, a liquid fuel. Natural gas occurs naturally. Gasoline is obtained from petroleum (see FUEL; GAS; GASOLINE; HYDROCARBON; METHANE; PETROLEUM).

Natural gas is found all over the world. However, half of all known deposits are in the United States and Russia. In nature, natural gas is odorless. A scent is added when natural gas is used for fuel, making it easier for people to detect leaks. Natural gas is used for fuel in homes and industry.

When natural gas is burned, the hydrocarbons it contains break down into individual hydrogen and carbon atoms. These atoms then combine with oxygen in the air to form water and carbon dioxide. These chemical reactions release heat, which can be used to heat a home or run the machines in a factory. Sometimes, the flame that comes from burning natural gas is used directly, as in gas stoves. One cu. ft. [0.0283 cu. m] of gas produces 252,000 calories of heat energy (see CALORIE). Natural gas produces very little pollution when burned.

Natural gas formation Natural gas was formed in much the same way as coal (see COAL). During the Carboniferous period, which began about 363 million years ago, the earth was covered with swamplike seas where gigantic plants grew (see CARBONIFEROUS PERIOD). As these plants died, they sank into the swamp. They were gradually covered by sediment and decayed (see DECOMPOSITION). New plants grew. The cycle repeated again until there were many layers of decayed matter. Great pressure was produced by the many layers. This pressure, combined with chemical reactions, changed the layers of decayed matter into natural gas. Once the decayed matter had been transformed into natural gas, it drained into pore-filled rocks. These rocks were gradually covered by more solid rock that trapped the gas. Because coal and natural gas formed in much the same way, they are often found together. Natural gas is also often found along with petroleum, which formed in much the same way.

Natural gas processing Scientists use different methods, called prospecting, to search for natural gas. For example, scientists may suspect that an area contains natural gas because of certain rock formations. A geologist (scientist who studies the earth) may then take sample rocks from the area. He or she tests the sample rocks to see if they contain certain fossils that would indicate natural gas may have formed there (see FOSSIL). Another prospecting method is to set off explosions underground. Scientists record the path of the waves caused by the explosion on an instrument called a seismograph. Scientists study the waves to determine underground rock formations (see PROSPECTING; SEISMOLOGY).

NATURAL GAS

Much natural gas is found in underground deposits offshore. It is extracted using rigs moored in shallow water. It is then pumped along pipelines to the shore.

Once scientists believe natural gas is present in an area, they drill test wells. If these test wells produce natural gas, the next step is to collect the gas by drilling (see DRILLING). The most common way to drill for natural gas is by rotary drilling. In rotary drilling, a tough bit with a diamond tip is rotated at the end of a long pipe. Once natural gas has been drilled for, it is carried from the well by a pipe called a gathering line to a facility called an extraction unit. There, chemicals that might cause the gas to burn less efficiently are removed. The natural gas is then piped to processing plants where other chemicals that are not needed are removed. After processing, the natural gas is carried to communities and then to individual homes and factories through a network of pipes. There are over two million miles [3,218,000 km] of natural gas pipes in the United States. Natural gas that is not needed immediately is stored in tanks above and below ground. It can be stored as a gas or converted to and stored as a liquid.

See also ENERGY; OIL RIG.

NATURAL RESOURCE

A natural resource is anything in, on, or above the earth that people use to meet their needs. People do not make natural resources but often collect them to use them. Air, minerals, soil, trees, and water are all examples of natural resources. Different areas have different natural resources. For example, Oregon has many trees. Illinois has good soil for crops. California and Florida have warm weather that is excellent for growing fruits and vegetables.

Some resources are renewable. This means that when some of the resource is used, it can be replaced. Trees are renewable because more can be grown. However, renewable resources have to be managed so they are not used up faster than they can be renewed. For example, it can take as long as two hundred years to replace a forest. It is important, then, that existing forests not be overcut (see DEFORESTATION; FORESTRY). Other resources are nonrenewable (see NONRENEWABLE RESOURCES).

Recycling helps conserve natural resources. Recycling involves collecting wastes and processing the materials that they contain in order to reuse the materials. Recycling paper products saves trees. Aluminum cans can be recycled into new aluminum products. Used motor oil can be cleaned and used again. However, recycling cannot solve all problems related to natural resources. For example, oil that has been spilled onto the ground or in the water cannot be gathered for reuse. Large areas of oceans and coastal areas have been damaged by oil that has accidentally spilled from large tanker ships or offshore wells.

See also CONSERVATION; POLLUTION; RECYCLING.

NATURAL RESOURCE

Commercial fishing (top) makes use of a natural resource of the oceans. So long as people do not catch too many fish, this resource is renewable. The plant (bottom) is refining crude oil. Oil is not a renewable resource. When all the oil is used up, it cannot be replaced.

NATURAL SELECTION

Natural selection is the process that most scientists believe has been responsible for directing the course of evolution and causing living things to become better adapted to their environments (see EVOLUTION). It was first suggested by the famous British naturalist Charles Darwin (see DARWIN, CHARLES). He realized that plants and animals usually produce many offspring, but that only the strongest or fittest survive in each generation. Darwin summed up these observations in two famous phrases—"the struggle for existence" and "the survival of the fittest." Natural selection is, as the name suggests, a natural process in which the environment, including predators and other competitors, weeds out the less fit individuals (see ENVIRONMENT). Only those best suited to the conditions and surroundings can survive and breed, and they pass on their "fitness" to their offspring. "Fitness" may include extra speed to catch food or escape enemies, better resistance to cold or drought, or better camouflage to hide from predators.

Because the environment differs from place to place, natural selection can act quite differently on two populations of the same species, causing them to evolve in two different directions and to produce two different species. Also, if two different animals live in similar conditions or environments, possibly in widely separated parts of the world, natural selection can cause them to evolve similar features. This happened with the ostrich in Africa and the rhea in South America. Both birds are adapted for a running life on the grasslands.

The way in which natural selection works to adapt organisms to their environments can be explained in connection with the wonderful examples of camouflage seen in the animal world today.

Suppose an insect population living thousands of years ago contained just a

DIVERSE BIRDS

The different species of honeycreepers on the Hawaiian Islands today all evolved from one original species. They can be divided into three groups: those with beaks adapted for eating (1) insects, (2) insects and nectar, and (3) seeds.

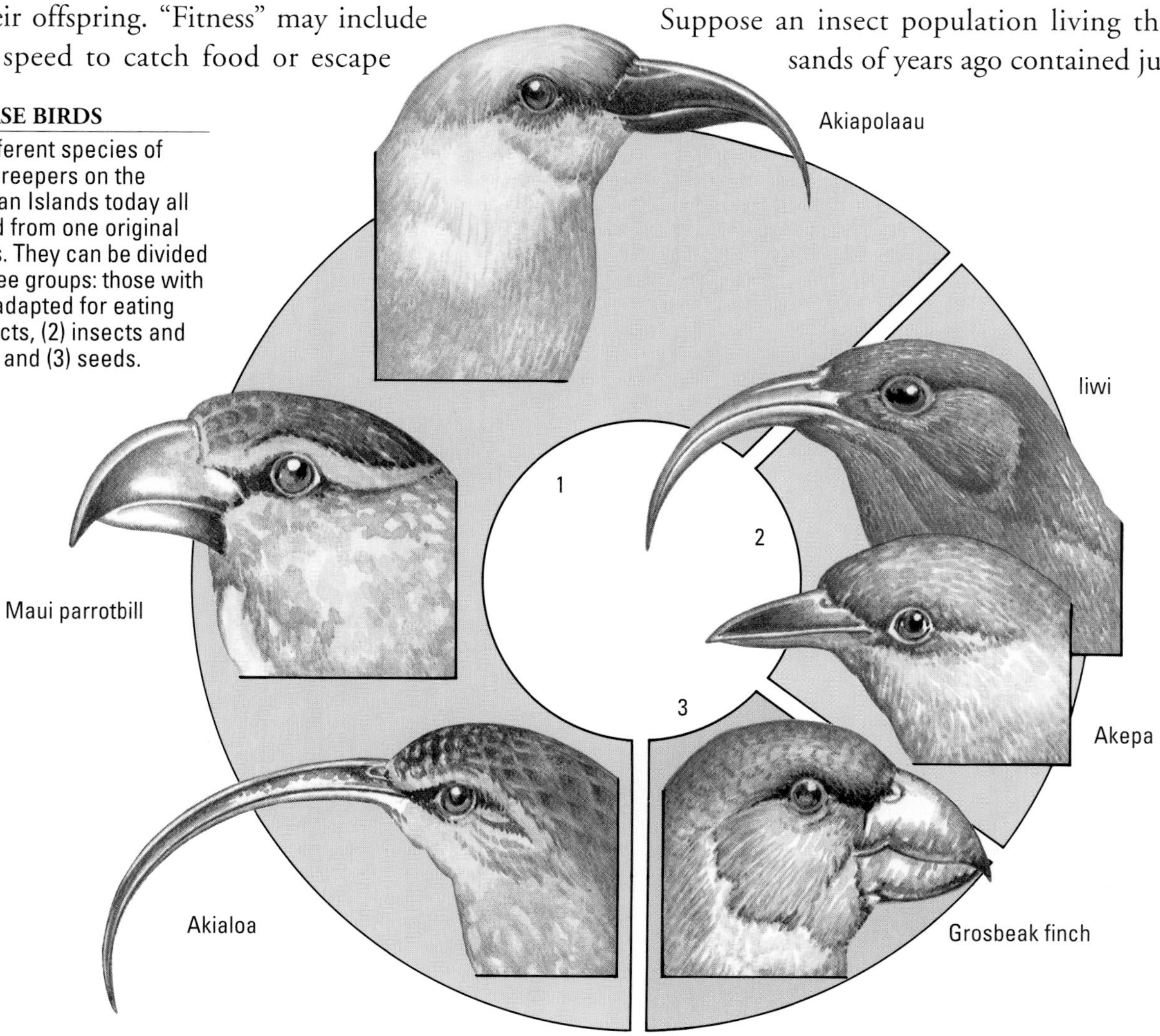

Akiapolaau

Iiwi

Maui parrotbill

Akepa

Akialoa

Grosbeak finch

few individuals that happened to look a bit more leaflike than the rest. This small difference could have caused birds and other predators to miss some of the leaflike insects and allow them to breed. Because individuals always vary a little, the next generation would also have contained some insects that were more leaflike than the rest. The process would have been repeated, with predators finding and eating the less well-camouflaged insects—the less "fit" ones—and allowing the better-camouflaged ones to survive. Tiny improvements in each generation would all add up, and after thousands of generations, they could easily have produced the amazing leaf insects and other leaflike insects that exist today (see LEAF INSECT).

Natural selection is still occurring. When trees and buildings became blackened with soot during the Industrial Revolution (late 1700s and 1800s) in Europe, the peppered moth population began to change (see PEPPERED MOTH). The original speckled black-and-white form began to be replaced by a black or melanic form that had not been seen before—although it undoubtedly did exist in small numbers. The change occurred because birds could easily see the speckled forms resting on the trees and buildings, but they could

not see the black ones. Now that pollution is controlled and trees and buildings are cleaner, the change is being reversed and the speckled moths are becoming more common. Some experiments carried out in the 1950s by British biologist Bernard Kettlewell provided convincing evidence that the changes have come about by natural selection. He put both black and speckled forms of the peppered moth on lichen-covered tree trunks. Almost all of the black forms were discovered and eaten by birds, while the speckled forms remained largely unseen and unharmed. When the experiments were tried on smoke-blackened trees, the speckled moths were eaten, and the black ones survived.

GIRAFFE EVOLUTION
Darwin's theory of natural selection explains why giraffes have long necks. The giraffe's ancestors (left) had short necks. Giraffes with chance mutations resulting in longer necks (center) got more food than short-necked rivals; they survived, and their offspring inherited long necks. Continued competition led to better survival by animals with very long necks (right).

Navigation is the science of finding the position and directing the movement of a craft from one point to another. The word *navigate* comes from two Latin words—*navis,* meaning "ship," and *agere,* meaning "to direct." All navigators (people who navigate), whether on land, on the sea, in the air, or in space, have to find their position and determine the direction in which they want to travel.

A brief history Early sea navigators sailed without instruments. They moved chiefly from point to point along coasts, always trying to keep within sight of land. It was very dangerous to go out into the open sea.

The invention of the astrolabe was a tremendous help to early navigators. The astrolabe made it possible for the navigator to measure roughly the angle between the horizon and heavenly bodies (see ASTROLABE).

Sometime around A.D. 1000 to A.D. 1200, the magnetic compass was being used by Chinese sailors. By using the compass, navigators could set a course for the direction in which they wished to go (see COMPASS).

In the 1700s, the invention of the accurate chronometer (to tell time) and the sextant (to measure angles) made it possible for navigators to know exactly where they were, even when far from land (see CHRONOMETER).

Methods and instruments Navigators on ships and aircraft often use algebra, geometry, and trigonometry to find out where they are in relation to landmarks and stars. Various navigational aids and instruments are used to get information about time, direction, distance, speed, and position. The techniques of navigation are piloting, dead reckoning, celestial navigation, and electronic navigation. These methods are often used in combination with each other. Piloting is simply a means of navigating by watching out for landmarks. Ship navigators use piloting when close to land. They watch for lighthouses, buoys, and other landmarks. An air navigator may check his or her position by using such landmarks as rivers and bridges. Piloting is called "contact flying" by airplane pilots.

Dead reckoning is a way of estimating direction and distance from a known position. Suppose a ship leaves New York harbor at 2 P.M. The ship's course is east. Its speed is 20 mi. [32.2 km] per hour. At 5 P.M., the navigator checks the direction of the ship, how long the ship has been sailing, and its speed. Then he or she may reckon (guess) that

COMPASS
The compass was one of the earliest aids to navigation. It is still one of the most important, especially on small seagoing vessels.

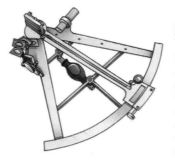

SEXTANT
The sextant allows a navigator to measure the angle of the sun or certain stars above the horizon. Using a sextant and a chronometer to tell the exact time, the navigator can then calculate the ship's position.

the ship is 60 mi. [96.5 km] east of New York. Dead reckoning is not exact, but is accurate enough for many purposes.

Celestial navigation is a way to check a position by observing the sun, other stars, moon, and planets. Celestial navigation makes use of the fact that these heavenly bodies are always in certain positions depending on the time of day or night and the date of the year. The navigator uses a sextant. A sextant measures the angle between a heavenly body and the horizon. When the navigator knows this angle, he or she looks up the heavenly body in a book that gives the exact position of each heavenly body at exact dates and times. From the body's angle, the date, and time, the navigator calculates the craft's position.

Navigators today generally use electronic systems to help them find their position. These systems involve such devices as radio sets, radar sets, and communications satellites (see ELECTRONICS; RADAR; RADIO; SATELLITE). Radio signals broadcast from special towers at airports help airplane pilots navigate. When the pilot is on the airway (the route airplanes fly from airport to airport), he or she hears a special hum. If the pilot goes off course, he or she hears a series of beeps. Radar is used by ocean-crossing airplanes in long-range navigation. Two radar units several miles or kilometers apart on land send a signal out to sea. The signals show up as two dots of light on the airplane's radar screen. The navigator turns a dial until the two dots become one, showing the airplane's position. A more recently developed system makes use of satellites that orbit Earth. Each satellite has a radio transmitter. The navigator tunes in the "beep" from a satellite. He or she then uses a special computer to measure the angle between the satellite and the ship or plane. The computer then figures out the position of the ship or plane.

Determining the position of a spacecraft is different from determining the postion of a ship or plane. For example, when a ship sails the ocean, the place the ship started from and the place it is going to do not move around with relation to each other. However, when astronauts blasted off for the moon, for example, the earth and the moon were both moving. In order for astronauts to find their way to and from the moon, they had a special sextant telescope aboard the spacecraft. This instrument measured the angle between the earth and a star and then gave this information to a computer. The computer, in turn, worked out the spacecraft's position (see SPACE EXPLORATION).

Scientists have even developed a navigation system for the time when manned spacecraft will travel to other planets in the solar system. Space navigation is called astrogation. The navigator, called an astrogator, will need a special almanac with tables giving the positions of planets in relation to the sun at any given time. The astrogator would measure the angle between the sun and the two closest planets. He or she would then compute his or her distance from the sun using geometry.

Getting from here to there Knowing the craft's position is the first half of a navigator's job. The second half involves getting the craft where it is supposed to go. For example, a navigator on a ship must first make sure that all the necessary tools and instruments are aboard. Once the ship leaves the harbor, the navigator finds out the ship's position and the exact time. This is called the point of departure. For example, the point of departure may be the moment when a ship passes a buoy. The navigator, noting the time, marks a small circle on a map called a chart.

The navigator then uses the chart to plot a course, or the path to a specific location. A network of imaginary lines, called latitudes and longitudes, is on each chart. Lines of longitude run north and south. Lines of latitude run east and west. Each point on the earth has its own position in terms of latitude and longitude (see LATITUDE AND LONGITUDE). Knowing his or her position, the navigator draws a line showing the planned course. The course is seldom a straight line. Ships must avoid storms and sail around islands. At every planned change of course, the navigator must measure his or her new position and set a new course. The navigator must have training in meteorology (weather science) and be able to read weather instruments. The navigator also checks the depth of the water with an instrument called a fathometer. From time to time during the voyage, the navigator uses all four basic methods of navigation.

The first land sighted after a voyage is called the landfall. The navigator checks the landfall on the chart to make sure he or she has navigated accurately. Again, the navigator uses the fathometer to check

the depth of the water to avoid going aground as the ship enters the harbor.

PROJECT 28

NAVIGATIONAL SATELLITE

A navigational satellite sends out a series of short radio signals. With the aid of a computer, the navigator tunes in to the signals and measures the angle between the satellite and the ship or airplane, and the computer then calculates its position.

NEANDERTHAL
Neanderthal people had prominent eyebrows and broad foreheads. They were hunters who used animal bones as simple tools. They also had rituals to bury their dead.

NEANDERTHAL (nē ăn' dər thôl') Neanderthal people were early human beings. They lived about 200,000 years ago and disappeared about 60,000 years ago with the coming of the Cro-Magnons (see CRO-MAGNON). Neanderthal people are named for the Neander Gorge in Germany, where their fossils were first discovered in 1856 (see FOSSIL).

Neanderthal people stood about 5 ft. 2 in. [157 cm] high and walked erect. They had powerful bones and strong teeth. Their brains were equal in size to the brains of modern people. Neanderthal culture was unique. The Neanderthals had rituals to bury their dead. Their religion is believed to be centered around the now-extinct cave bear.

Fossils of Neanderthal people have been found in Europe, Asia, and Africa. Simple tools and animal bones were discovered near the European site, supporting the theory that Neanderthal people were hunters. Neanderthal people probably lived in makeshift shelters and caves and practiced a primitive form of religion.

See also HUMAN BEING.

NEAP TIDE Neap tides, which occur twice a month, are tides that do not rise as high as normal tides. Tides are caused by the gravitational pull of the earth, the moon, and the sun, all acting on the water of the ocean. During the first and third quarters of the moon, the pull of the sun is at right angles to the pull of the moon, resulting in neap tides.

See also MOON; TIDE.

NEAP TIDE
At new moon and full moon, the gravitational pulls of the sun and the moon line up and result in a very high tide called a spring tide. Less high tides, called neap tides, occur at the first and third quarters of the moon, when the pulls of the sun and moon are at right angles.

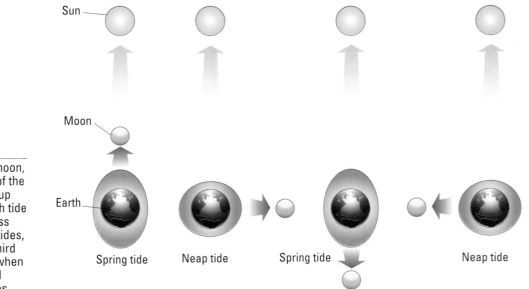

Sun

Moon

Earth

Spring tide   Neap tide   Spring tide   Neap tide

NEBULA (nĕb′ yə lə) A nebula is a large cloud of gases and dust in outer space. The name *nebula* comes from the Latin word meaning "cloud." There are two main types of nebulae (plural of *nebula*): diffuse nebulae and planetary nebulae.

Diffuse nebulae are much larger than planetary nebulae. Sometimes, a diffuse nebula is close enough to a star so that dust in the nebula reflects the starlight. This type of nebula is called a reflective nebula.

A diffuse nebula sometimes receives energy from a powerful star that is nearby. The nebula then begins to emit its own radiation. Such a nebula is called an emission nebula (see RADIATION).

Diffuse nebulae may occur in a region of outer space where there are no nearby stars. The dust in the nebula may block out or partly obscure the stars behind it. This type of diffuse nebula is called a dark nebula.

A planetary nebula is an expanding cloud of glowing gas that surrounds a star. A planetary nebula emits radiation in the same way as an emission nebula—radiation from the central star causes it to glow. All planetary nebulae are expanding and are

NEBULA

The Horsehead Nebula is a large cloud of dust and gas in outer space that is shaped like a horse's head. It can be seen in the constellation of Orion.

probably material ejected from the central star. *See also* STAR.

NECTARINE The nectarine is a smooth-skinned variety of peach. The nectarine tree is a member of the rose family, Rosaceae. Nectarines and peaches have identical tree and leaf characteristics. Both require the same kind of soil and climate for successful cultivation.

The flesh of the nectarine may be red, yellow, or white. Nectarines are rich in vitamins A and C. *See also* FRUIT; PEACH; ROSE FAMILY.

NEGATIVE NUMBER During subtraction, one number is taken away from another number. For example, subtracting 2 from 5 leaves 3. This is written as 5 - 2 = 3. Suppose that the second number is bigger than the first. For example, in the subtraction 5 - 7, the second number is bigger than the first. The answer is called negative 2 and is an example of a negative number. The equation is written as 5 - 7 = -2. Two negative numbers can be added together to give another negative number: -2 + (-3) = -5. When two negative numbers are multiplied together, they give a positive number: -2 x (-3) = 6. Negative numbers are usually integers (whole numbers).

See also EQUATION; NUMBER.

NEKTON (něk´ tən) Nekton is the collective name given to organisms that swim freely in the sea. Fish, whales, seals, squid, and prawns are all nekton. Organisms that drift in the sea currents are called plankton. Organisms that live on or in the sea floor are called benthos. Some organisms belong to the benthos at one time in their lives, plankton at another, and nekton at another time.

See also BENTHOS; PLANKTON.

NEMATODE (něm´ ə tōd´) A nematode is a slender, round worm. Although nematodes have sometimes been listed as a class within the phylum Aschelminthes, they are generally treated as a separate phylum, Nematoda. Some nematodes are so small they can be seen only with a microscope. Most grow to be 0.04 to 2 in. [1 mm to 5 cm] long, although some are over 12 in. [30 cm] long. A nematode's body is usually pointed at both ends. Males are smaller than females.

Some nematodes live in soil and water. Many, such as the eelworm and the root-knot nematode, live as parasites in plants. Hookworms, lungworms, pinworms, trichinas, and filarias live as parasites in human beings. They also live in dogs, sheep, and horses.

Nematodes are abundant everywhere in the world. They are almost as numerous as insects. Humans try to control the number of parasitic nematodes using various methods, such as pesticides. Pesticides

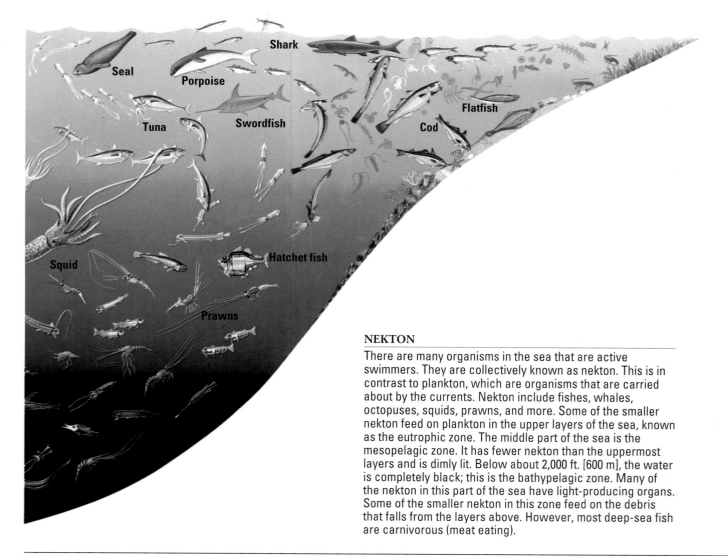

Seal · Porpoise · Shark · Tuna · Swordfish · Cod · Flatfish · Squid · Hatchet fish · Prawns

NEKTON

There are many organisms in the sea that are active swimmers. They are collectively known as nekton. This is in contrast to plankton, which are organisms that are carried about by the currents. Nekton include fishes, whales, octopuses, squids, prawns, and more. Some of the smaller nekton feed on plankton in the upper layers of the sea, known as the eutrophic zone. The middle part of the sea is the mesopelagic zone. It has fewer nekton than the uppermost layers and is dimly lit. Below about 2,000 ft. [600 m], the water is completely black; this is the bathypelagic zone. Many of the nekton in this part of the sea have light-producing organs. Some of the smaller nekton in this zone feed on the debris that falls from the layers above. However, most deep-sea fish are carnivorous (meat eating).

NEMATODE

A roundworm is a typical nematode. Roundworms "stab" their food with a spikelike stylet sticking out of the mouth. Most live as parasites in animals or plants. The female (shown here) has large ovaries that produce hundreds of eggs.

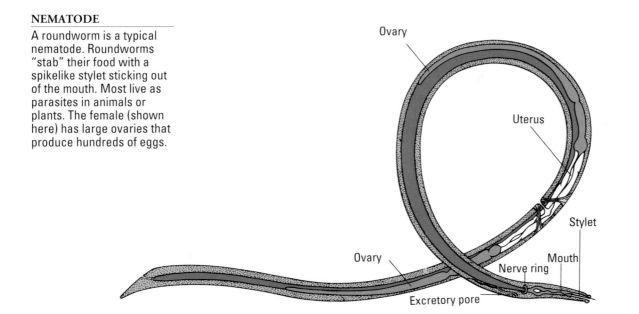

used to control nematodes are called nematocides. *See also* PARASITE; PESTICIDE; WORM.

NEON Neon (Ne) is a gaseous element with no odor or color. Neon is one of the inert gases (see ELEMENT; INERT GAS). This means that it is very unreactive. Only a few compounds of neon are known (see COMPOUND). Neon was discovered by the British chemist Sir William Ramsay in 1898 (see RAMSAY, SIR WILLIAM).

Neon occurs in small amounts in the air. In 35.3 cu. ft. [1 cu. m] of air, there are about 0.7 cu. in. [18 cu. mm] of neon. Neon is obtained by liquefying air. When something is liquefied, it is reduced to its liquid state. The liquefied air is then allowed to boil. The neon is separated from the other gases in the air by a process called distillation (see DISTILLATION). Most neon is used in neon advertising signs. If electricity is passed through neon, it glows a bright orange red. If a little mercury is added, the color changes to green or blue. Neon is also used in navigation lights and beacons (see ELECTRIC LIGHT).

Neon's atomic number is 10, and its relative atomic mass is 20.179. Neon boils at -410.8°F [-246°C] and freezes at -415.7°F [-248.7°C].

NEOPRENE (nē′ ə prēn′) Neoprene is a kind of artificial rubber made from a substance called chloroprene. Neoprene is sometimes called polychloroprene. Large numbers of molecules of chloroprene are joined together in a chain to form one molecule of neoprene. This process is called polymerization (see POLYMERIZATION). Neoprene resists corrosion by the air better than natural rubber. It cannot be used at very low temperatures. *See also* CORROSION; RUBBER.

NEON

Neon tubes can be shaped in almost any way to produce attention-getting displays.

NEPTUNE

Neptune is currently the ninth planet from the sun. Neptune became the ninth planet in 1976, when Pluto became closer to the sun. On March 13, 1999, Pluto will once again be the most distant planet from the sun. Neptune will return to its position as the eighth planet. Neptune is named for the Roman sea god Neptune. Neptune and Pluto are the only known planets of the solar system that cannot be seen by the unaided eye. Astronomers have learned more about Neptune since the space probe *Voyager 2* passed by it in 1989 (see PLANET; SOLAR SYSTEM; SPACE EXPLORATION).

Neptune has a diameter of 30,760 mi. [49,500 km]. The planet orbits the sun every 165 years, following an elliptical (oval-shaped) path. Its orbit averages about 2,795 million mi. [4,498 million km] from the sun. Neptune makes one complete rotation (spin) on its axis (an imaginary line running through its center) every 16 to 28 hours.

Neptune's atmosphere is mainly composed of hydrogen and helium, with traces of methane and ammonia. Methane gives the planet its bluish green color. Winds blow very strongly in Neptune's atmosphere. Winds blowing at 1,500 m.p.h. [2,414 kph] have been recorded. These are the strongest recorded winds of any planet in the solar

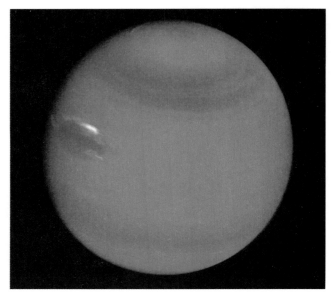

BLUE PLANET

This view of Neptune was taken by cameras on board the *Voyager 2* space probe. It shows bright clouds high in the planet's atmosphere. The atmosphere contains methane gas, which causes the blue color.

system (see SOLAR SYSTEM). Several large dark spots are present in Neptune's atmosphere. These spots are actually huge storms that spin in a counterclockwise direction. These dark spots are similar to Jupiter's famous red spot (see JUPITER). The largest of Neptune's spots, "The Great Dark Spot," is about the size of Earth. Bright clouds appear to

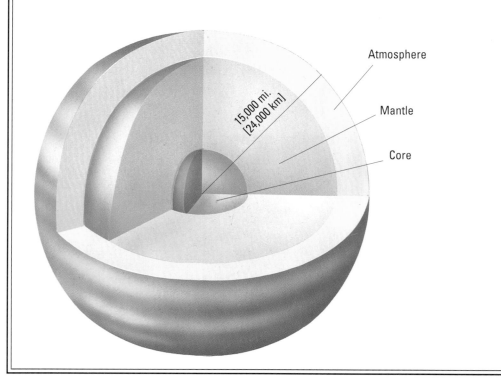

15,000 mi. [24,000 km]

Atmosphere

Mantle

Core

NEPTUNE STRUCTURE

Neptune has a small core made of iron and silicate, surrounded by a mantle of liquid or solid gases. The atmosphere forms the outer layer. It consists mainly of hydrogen and helium, with some methane and ammonia.

form high in Neptune's atmosphere. Temperatures vary greatly in Neptune's atmosphere, ranging from 900°F [882°C] to -360°F [-218°C].

Neptune has eight known satellites, or moons (see SATELLITE). Two of Neptune's moons, Triton and Nereid, were known before *Voyager 2* passed by. *Voyager 2* discovered six other moons circling the planet. Triton is Neptune's largest moon. Triton has a diameter of 1,680 mi. [2,703 km]. It orbits Neptune every 6 days. Triton has cliffs, craters, and faults, or cracks, in its surface. Scientists think that these landforms occurred because Triton froze, melted, and then refroze time after time. *Voyager 2* also showed geyserlike eruptions on Triton (see SPRING AND GEYSER). These eruptions spew nitrogen and dust particles. Nereid is much smaller than

Triton. It has a diameter of 211 mi. [339 km]. Nereid orbits Neptune every 360 days. Very little else is known about Nereid or the other six moons.

Voyager 2 also sent back information about rings around Neptune. Until that time, scientists had never seen rings around Neptune. Neptune is circled by four complete and several incomplete rings.

Neptune was mathematically predicted to exist before it was actually discovered. John Couch Adams, an English astronomer and mathematician, predicted Neptune's existence in 1845. Neptune was first seen through a telescope in 1846.

ICY MOON

Triton is the largest of Neptune's eight moons. Astronomers think that Triton has melted and refrozen many times. This view shows Neptune "rising" over Triton's icy landscape.

NERVE CELL A nerve cell is a cell that carries messages (see CELL). The messages are in the form of electric signals, called nerve impulses. Nerve impulses travel through the cell and are passed on to other cells. Millions and millions of nerve cells linked together make up the nervous system (see NERVOUS SYSTEM). One part of the nervous system, the brain, contains about ten billion nerve cells (see BRAIN). The nerve cells help form a vast, highly complex communications network.

Another term for nerve cell is *neuron.* There are many different sizes and shapes of neurons. However, all neurons have the same basic parts. All neurons have a cell body. The cell body is wider than the other parts of the cell. The cell body contains the nucleus, which is the neuron's control center for growth and other activities. From the cell body, numerous branches spread out and meet the branches of other nerve cells.

The branches that carry messages or impulses toward the cell body are called dendrites. The branch that carries messages away from the cell body is called the axon. In some neurons, the axon is very small. In others, the axon may be over 3 ft. [1 m] long. The main nerves of the body are made of bundles of axons.

When a nerve impulse spreads along a neuron, it travels along the thin membrane at the surface of the cell (see MEMBRANE). There is normally a differ-ence of electric charge between the neuron inside the membrane and the outside of the membrane. This is partly because there are more potassium ions inside and more sodium ions outside. They do not balance (see IONS AND IONIZATION). When the membrane is stimulated by a nerve impulse, the arrangement of the molecules of the membrane is changed, and ions can pass through. Potassium ions rush out, and sodium ions rush in. This means that the electric charge of the neuron changes. This change in charge affects the arrangement of mole-cules in the membrane of a neuron nearby. In other words, the nerve impulse spreads to the nearby neu-ron. Because the neurons do not actually touch each other, the impulse has to jump across the tiny gap between the neurons, called a synapse (see SYNAPSE). As the nerve impulse reaches the synapse, it causes the release of a chemical called a transmitter into the tiny gap. The chemical passes across the gap and stimulates the membrane of the nearby cell. This causes the nearby cell's membrane to let some of its potassium ions rush out and some sodium ions rush in, and the impulse continues its journey.

Nerve impulses travel at different speeds in dif-ferent kinds of neurons. Thick neurons conduct signals very quickly, up to 328 ft. [100 m] per sec-ond. Such neurons have branches covered with a sheath of a fatty substance called myelin. Thin neu-rons with uncovered branches may conduct impulses at only 3 ft. [1 m] per second.

Neurons have different types of functions. Receptor neurons are found in the sense organs, such as the eyes. They translate such stimuli as light into messages (see RECEPTOR; SENSE). These mes-sages are carried to the central nervous system by sensory neurons. Neurons that carry messages from the central nervous system to muscles, telling them to contract, and to glands, telling them to produce their secretions, are called motor neurons. There are also many neurons that carry messages from one place to another within the brain itself.

Unlike most other cells in the body, nerve cells cannot be replaced when they die or are acci-dentally destroyed. This is why injury to the brain, or interruption of its blood supply, is so dangerous. PROJECT 71

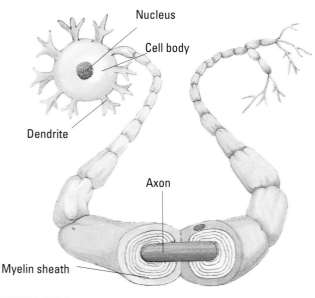

NERVE CELL

The diagram above shows the structure of a nerve cell, or neuron. A long axon extends from the body of the cell. The fatty substance myelin surrounds and insulates the axon.

Nervous System

The nervous system is a system for passing signals from one part of the body to another. All but the smallest and simplest of organisms have special cells to do this. The cells are called nerve cells, or neurons (see NERVE CELL). Linked together, they form an internal communications network.

In the invertebrates (animals without backbones), there may be only a few nerve cells linked together. Highly developed invertebrates have knots of neurons in different parts of the body, called ganglia (plural of *ganglion*). At each ganglion, messages are exchanged and travel onward along different routes. In the earthworm, a ganglion at the front of the body is bigger than the others. The earthworm's ganglion represents the simplest form of brain.

In the vertebrates (animals with backbones), the nervous system is more complicated. Vertebrates have a brain, which is made of millions of nerve cells linked together; a spinal cord; and nerves that communicate with all parts of the body. Humans have the most highly developed nervous system of all organisms, with billions of nerve cells (see BRAIN; SPINAL CORD).

The human nervous system is divided into two main parts. The brain and the spinal cord are the controlling parts. Together, they are called the central nervous system. The brain is protected by the bones of the skull (see SKULL). The spinal cord is protected by the bones of the spinal column (see VERTEBRA). From the brain and spinal cord, nerves (cordlike bundles of neuron fibers) extend to all parts of the body. These nerves make up the peripheral nervous system.

Another way to divide the nervous system is by the work that different neurons do. In the voluntary nervous system, the nerves are all concerned with conscious sensations. They carry out instructions given by the brain that are directed by will. For example, when a person wants to walk, write,

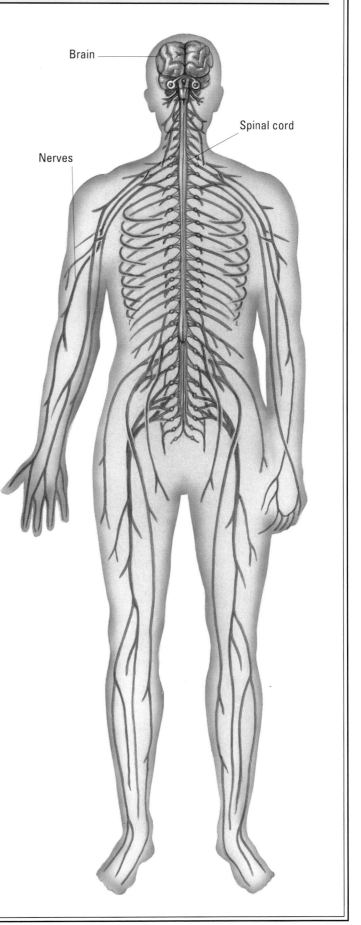

Brain

Spinal cord

Nerves

HUMAN NERVOUS SYSTEM

The brain and spinal cord make up the central nervous system. Nerves that branch off the brain and spinal cord make up the peripheral nervous system.

or talk, he or she uses the neurons of the voluntary nervous system. The neurons of the autonomic system are the ones that carry out unconscious activities. For example, the autonomic nervous system regulates the rate of the heartbeat and controls the speed of digestion.

The autonomic nervous system can be further divided into the sympathetic and parasympathetic systems. The activities of each of these systems balance one another. For example, nerve impulses in the sympathetic system tend to increase heart rate and blood pressure. Nerve impulses in the parasympathetic nervous system tend to have the opposite effect. As conditions change, the two systems trade control of unconscious activities.

It is possible to control some of the activities of the autonomic nervous system using biofeedback (see BIOFEEDBACK). PROJECT 71

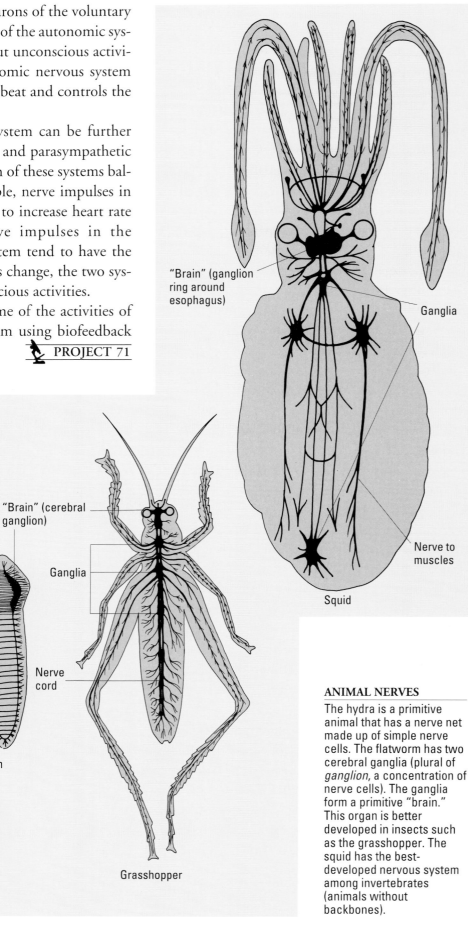

"Brain" (ganglion ring around esophagus)

Ganglia

Nerve to muscles

Squid

"Brain" (cerebral ganglion)

Ganglia

Nerve cord

Nerve cord

Nerve cord

Hydra

Flatworm

Grasshopper

ANIMAL NERVES
The hydra is a primitive animal that has a nerve net made up of simple nerve cells. The flatworm has two cerebral ganglia (plural of *ganglion*, a concentration of nerve cells). The ganglia form a primitive "brain." This organ is better developed in insects such as the grasshopper. The squid has the best-developed nervous system among invertebrates (animals without backbones).

NETTLE FAMILY The nettle family, Urticaceae, contains about 500 species of herbs and small shrubs. The best-known species is the common stinging nettle, which, like many of its relatives, is clothed with stinging hairs.

The hairs contain formic acid, which causes a bothersome itch if someone comes in contact with it. Some kinds of nettles are cooked and eaten, especially in Europe. Many contain strong fibers and are used to make cloths and rope. Other members of the family include ramie, a small bush yielding a valuable fiber.

NETTLE FAMILY
The common stinging nettle, shown here, has hairs containing formic acid, which causes a bothersome itch.

NEURAL NETWORK A neural network, also called a nerve net, is a simple kind of nervous system consisting of a network of nerve cells spreading through the body (see NERVE CELL; NERVOUS SYSTEM). Neural networks are found mainly in sea anemones and starfish and their relatives (see CNIDARIA; ECHINODERMATA; SEA ANEMONE; STARFISH). These animals have no real brain, and all of their activities are controlled by the neural network. Stimulation of one part of the body causes signals to pass from cell to cell through the network, and the animals react accordingly. For example, if a sea anemone's tentacles are lightly prodded, they contract (pull back) in the region of the disturbance. If the prodding is very strong or continued very long, the signals will travel farther across the nerve net and may result in the whole anemone closing up. In vertebrates and other animals with a well-developed brain and spinal cord, neural networks generally occur only in the walls of the digestive system. They control the rhythmic movements that push food through the system.

NEUTRALIZATION (nōō´ trə lĭ zā´ shən) Neutralization is a chemical reaction in which an acid and a base combine and form a salt and water (see CHEMICAL REACTION). The molecules of water consist of two atoms of hydrogen and one atom of oxygen. Water's formula is H_2O. A small number of water molecules are separated into hydrogen ions (H^+) and hydroxide ions (OH^-) (see ATOM; IONS AND IONIZATION; MOLECULE). Hydrogen ions have a positive electric charge, and hydroxide ions have a negative electric charge. Acid solutions contain more hydrogen ions than water does. Basic solutions, on the other hand, contain more hydroxide ions than water does (see ACID; BASE). When an acid solution combines with a basic solution, their hydrogen and hydroxide ions join to form water molecules. The acid is said to be neutralized by the base. When the acid is exactly neutralized, the solution has the same number of hydrogen ions and hydroxide ions as water.

During neutralization, an acid and base form a salt as well as water. The salt in the water is in solution (see SALTS; SOLUTION AND SOLUBILITY). When the salt and base are of equal strength, the solution is neutral. A salt formed by the neutralization of a strong acid by a weak base is acidic. A salt formed by the neutralization of a weak acid with a strong base is basic.

See also NEUTRAL STATE.　　　PROJECT 1

NEUTRAL STATE The word *neutral* has different meanings in chemistry and in physics, though there is some overlap between the two. In chemistry, a substance is neutral if it is neither acidic nor basic (see ACID; BASE; NEUTRALIZATION). For example, pure water is a neutral substance.

In physics, a neutral state means an absence of electric charge. There are two kinds of electric charge: positive and negative. Suppose an object has a positive charge. Then it can be neutralized by adding a negative charge. The amount of negative charge added has to be equal to its positive charge. The object is then neutral.

See also CHARGE.

NEUTRINO (noo trē′ nō) Neutrinos are especially tiny subatomic particles. A subatomic particle is a particle smaller than an atom (see ATOM). Neutrinos belong to the group of subatomic particles called leptons (see PARTICLE PHYSICS).

There are more neutrinos than any other kind of particle in the universe. Neutrinos have much less mass than an electron and probably none at all when at rest (see ELECTRON; MASS). They travel at nearly the speed of light. Neutrinos spin as they move, similar to a football when it is thrown.

Neutrinos are able to pass through the earth without stopping or slowing. This makes them difficult to detect. The Austrian physicist Wolfgang Pauli first suggested that neutrinos exist (see PAULI, WOLFGANG). He made this suggestion in 1930 after studying a process called beta decay (see RADIOACTIVITY). In beta decay, the neutron in an atomic nucleus decays and gives off particles. Pauli suggested that one of these particles had spin but no mass. This particle was named the neutrino.

The existence of neutrinos was finally confirmed in 1956 using particle accelerators (see ACCELERATORS, PARTICLE). It is now known that the particle given off in beta decay is actually an antineutrino. An antineutrino is an antiparticle. Antiparticles are mirror images of their corresponding particles. They may have an opposite electric charge or an opposite direction of spin.

See also ANTIMATTER; ELEMENTARY PARTICLES.

NEUTRON An atom is made up of a central core called a nucleus, with a number of surrounding electrons. Most nuclei (plural of *nucleus*) are in turn made up of two main kinds of particles, protons and neutrons. Like the proton and the electron, the neutron is a very tiny particle. Like other particles that are smaller than atoms, the neutron is called a subatomic particle (see ATOM; ELECTRON; NUCLEUS; PROTON). According to current theory, the neutron is itself composed of even smaller particles, called quarks (see QUARK). Unlike the proton and the electron, the neutron has no electric charge. The mass of a neutron is slightly more than that of a proton (see MASS). The neutron was discovered in 1932 by an English physicist named Sir James Chadwick (see CHADWICK, SIR JAMES).

For a particular element, the number of protons in the nucleus is always the same. However, the number of neutrons in a nucleus can vary. Atoms of the same element that have different numbers of neutrons in their nuclei are called isotopes of that element (see ELEMENT; ISOTOPE). For example, the element oxygen always has eight protons in its nucleus. Most oxygen atoms also have eight neutrons in each nucleus. However, isotopes of oxygen exist that have nine or ten neutrons in their nuclei. Artificial isotopes can be made by firing beams of neutrons at elements. The nuclei in the atoms of the elements absorb the neutrons and become different isotopes. The extra neutrons usually make the nuclei unstable, and they become radioactive (see RADIOACTIVITY).

When a neutron is outside a nucleus, it is unstable. On average, a neutron decays in about fifteen minutes. This length of time is called the half-life of the neutron. Inside the nucleus, the neutrons are usually stable. When they decay inside the nucleus, the nucleus becomes radioactive.

Beams of neutrons are very dangerous because they can easily penetrate material. Scientists working in nuclear establishments have to be well protected from them.

See also HALF-LIFE; PARTICLE PHYSICS.

NEUTRON STAR A neutron star is an extremely small but very dense star made almost entirely of tightly compressed neutrons (see

NEUTRON). A neutron star is one of the final stages of a star's existence (see STAR).

A star that is more massive than the sun passes through several stages throughout its lifetime and then explodes. If the star throws off more than 10 percent of its matter, it is a supernova (see SUPERNOVA). If the mass of the remaining core of the supernova is between 1.4 and 2.5 times that of our sun, the supernova will develop into a neutron star. *See also* PULSAR.

NEWT A newt is a small animal that belongs to the salamander family, Salamandridae. Like all salamanders, newts are amphibians. There are many different species of newts. The newts common in North America average between 2 to 4 in. [5 to 10 cm] long. Newt larvae hatch from eggs in water. Unlike frog and toad larvae or tadpoles, newt larvae keep their feathery external gills until they leave the water. The young newts, called efts at this stage, stay on land for up to three years before returning to the water to breed (see LARVA). Like other salamanders, newts have long, slender bodies and four short legs. Most have smooth, slippery skin. They eat insects, frog eggs and tadpoles, and worms. Some newts have poisonous chemicals in their skin and are well protected from enemies, but others are eaten by a wide range of fish and other creatures.
See also AMPHIBIAN; SALAMANDER.

NEWTON The newton is the international system (SI) unit of force. In the customary system of measurement, force is measured in pounds (see FORCE; METRIC SYSTEM). A force of one newton gives a mass of 2.2 lb. [1 kg] an acceleration of 3.3 ft. per second per second [1 m per second per second]. The acceleration due to gravity is about 33 ft. per second per second [10 m per second per second]. Therefore, one newton is about equal to the pull of gravity on a weight of 3.5 oz. [100 g]. This is the weight of an average apple or a quarter-pound hamburger. The newton is named after the scientist Sir Isaac Newton.
See also ACCELERATION; GRAVITY; MASS; NEWTON, SIR ISAAC.

NEWT

Red-spotted newts (1), seen here in courtship display, are named for their red spots. The young red-spotted newt, or eft, (2) is red all over. The smooth newt (3) is duller in color, with black spots. It also has a crest along its body and tail.

NEWTON, SIR ISAAC (1642–1727) Sir

Isaac Newton was an English scientist and mathematician. He was one of the greatest scientists and mathematicians of all time. He made discoveries in mathematics, astronomy, mechanics, and optics (see ASTRONOMY; MATHEMATICS; MECHANICS; OPTICS).

His most famous discovery in mathematics was calculus (see CALCULUS). Calculus is a very useful technique for scientists. It can be used to solve a wide range of problems.

In astronomy, Newton discovered the law of universal gravitation. This law states that every body in the universe attracts every other body. The force of the attraction depends on their masses and on the distance between them. The force that keeps the planets in their orbits is gravity. Gravity also is the force that causes a body to fall to the ground. Newton was the first to realize that gravity is the same on the earth as it is in the rest of the universe. That is why he called his theory universal (see GRAVITY). Using his theory of universal gravitation, Newton calculated the shape of the orbits of the planets. He proved that the orbits were not quite circular. They are ellipses, or oval shaped. Other scientists had realized that this was true. However, Newton was the first to prove it mathematically (see PLANET).

Newton also made great contributions to the science of mechanics. His laws and theories of mechanics were published in 1687 in a book called *Philosophiae Naturali Principia Mathematica*. This famous book is usually called simply the *Principia*. It included his three laws of motion. These laws describe how forces affect the motion of a body (see DYNAMICS; MOTION, LAWS OF).

In optics, Newton experimented with prisms (see PRISM). He used a prism to split white light into its various colors. He was the first to suggest that white light is a mixture of different colors. He also built the first reflecting telescope (see TELESCOPE). His work on light and color was published in 1704 in a book called *Opticks*. Newton's theories on mechanics and gravity lasted for over two hundred years. It was only in this century that Albert Einstein proved that they were not quite accurate. He did this with his theory

of relativity (see EINSTEIN, ALBERT; RELATIVITY). However, Newton's theories are still accurate enough for most purposes. They are widely used today by scientists and engineers. ⚲ PROJECT 32, 46

SIR ISAAC NEWTON
The scientist and mathematician Sir Isaac Newton made discoveries in astronomy, physics, and mathematics.

NEWTON'S RINGS Suppose that a lens is

placed on a flat mirror. The lens has one side flat and the other side is curved in a convex shape (see CONVEX). The lens rests on its curved side. If light shines down through the lens, rings are seen in the lens. These rings are called Newton's rings because Sir Isaac Newton studied them in detail (see NEWTON, SIR ISAAC). When the beam of light passes through the lens, some of it is reflected (bounced off) from the bottom surface of the lens. The rest of the light passes through and is reflected off the mirror. The beam reflected off the mirror passes back through the lens. As it passes into the lens, it combines with the beam being reflected off the bottom surface of the lens. However, the beam reflected from the mirror has traveled a greater distance than the one reflected off the bottom of the lens. The beams may be out of step with each other. Light moves like waves, with definite wavelengths. A wavelength is the distance from the crest, or starting point, of one wave to the crest of the next (see FREQUENCY; WAVE). If the distance between the two beams of light is a whole number of wavelengths, and the waves are a certain distance from the center of the lens, their crests will come together. The

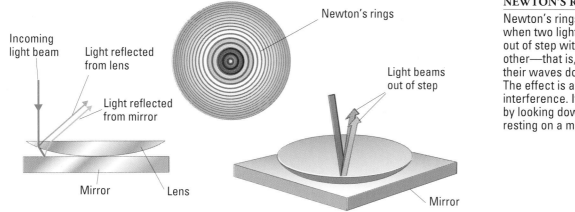

Newton's rings

Incoming light beam

Light reflected from lens

Light reflected from mirror

Mirror

Lens

Light beams out of step

Mirror

Newton's rings are formed when two light beams are out of step with each other—that is, the crests of their waves do not coincide. The effect is an example of interference. It can be seen by looking down on a lens resting on a mirror.

two beams will make each other stronger, and a bright ring will be seen. If the distance between the two beams is half a wavelength (or $1^1/_2$, $2^1/_2$, and so on), then they cancel out each other. This is called interference, and it produces a dark ring (see INTER-FERENCE).

Newton's rings are best seen if light of one color is used. White light is a mixture of different colors. It produces rings of different colors. For example, at certain distances from the center of the lens, the red light may cancel out. This causes a blue ring to be seen. At other distances, rings of different colors are formed.
See also COLOR.

NICHE (nĭch) The niche, or ecological niche, of an organism is the ecological role that the organism plays in its environment or community. The niche is similar to the microhabitat of the organism in some ways, but the niche is more than just the place where the organism lives. For example, two insects living under loose bark are sharing the same micro-habitat, but if one eats fungi and the other eats mites, the insects occupy different ecological niches. No two species can occupy the same niche. *See also* HABITAT.

NICKEL Nickel (Ni) is a hard, silvery white metal-lic element (see ELEMENT). Nickel was discovered

NICKEL
Powerful earth-moving machinery is used to take nickel ore from mines deep beneath the earth's surface. Most nickel is mixed with other metals to make alloys.

by Swedish chemist Axel Cronstedt in 1751. The chief mineral ore of nickel is pentlandite, a mixture of nickel, iron, and sulfur (see ORE). To obtain nickel, the ore is first heated. This changes the nickel compounds in the ore into nickel oxide (see COMPOUND; OXIDE). The oxide is then reacted with hydrogen to produce the metal nickel. Nickel obtained in this way is not very pure. It is purified by a method called the Mond process. In the Mond process, the nickel is treated with the gas carbon monoxide. This forms a compound called nickel carbonyl. The nickel carbonyl is then heated, and it decomposes (breaks down) into pure nickel.

Most nickel is used to make alloys (see ALLOY). Nickel alloys have many uses. Cupronickel is an alloy of copper and nickel. It is used to make coins. Nickel silver is an alloy of copper, nickel, and zinc. It is used for making cutlery (see NICKEL SILVER). Other nickel-copper alloys are used to prepare the tubing in desalination plants for converting seawater into fresh water. Invar is an alloy of iron and nickel. It expands very little with heat and is used to make rulers and mechanisms in clocks.

Nickel is magnetic and many compounds of nickel are green, so they are used for coloring glass. Compounds of nickel are also used in a process called electroplating. In this process, an object is coated with a very thin layer of nickel to provide protection.

Nickel's atomic number is 28, and its relative atomic mass is 58.69. It melts at 2,647°F [1,453°C] and boils at 4,950°F [2,732°C]. Its relative density is 8.9.
See also RELATIVE DENSITY.

NICKEL SILVER

Nickel silver is a silvery white alloy (see ALLOY). It contains the metals copper, nickel, and zinc (see COPPER; NICKEL; ZINC). It is also known as German silver. Nickel silver is widely used for cutlery. It has an attractive color, is easy to shape, and resists corrosion (see CORROSION). Cutlery made from nickel silver is often coated with a very thin layer of silver. Such cutlery has the letters *EPNS* stamped on it. This stands for *electroplated nickel silver*. The amount of nickel in nickel silver varies from 5 to 35 percent. The amount of copper is between 50 and 80 percent. The rest is zinc. The more nickel the metal contains, the whiter it is. Nickel silver with about 20 percent nickel is very springy. It is used for contacts in telephone equipment.

NICTITATING MEMBRANE (nĭk′ tĭ tāt′ ĭng mĕm′ brān′)

The nictitating membrane is a semitransparent fold of skin that can be pulled across the eyeball to keep it clean and moist. All birds and many reptiles and mammals have a nictitating membrane. Human beings do not have it.
See also EYE AND VISION.

NIGHTHAWK

The nighthawk is a bird that belongs to the goatsucker family, Caprimulgidae. It is not a hawk, despite its name (see HAWK). It is about 9 in. [22.5 cm] long with wings 22 in. [55 cm] long. The nighthawk is mostly brown with white patches on its wings and tail. It flies at night, catching insects for food. There are two species of nighthawks in North America. The common nighthawk is found throughout North America, even in large cities. The lesser nighthawk lives only in southwestern North America.
See also BIRD; NOCTURNAL BEHAVIOR.

NIGHTSHADE FAMILY

The nightshade family, Solanaceae, includes about two thousand species of herbaceous plants, shrubs, and tropical trees. Most of them are native to tropical America. They are dicotyledons and have alternate leaves. The flowers are star-shaped or trumpet-shaped due to the partial fusion (merging) of the five petals and the five sepals. The fruit is a berry (see BERRY; DICOTYLEDON; FLOWER; HERBACEOUS PLANT; LEAF; SHRUB).

Some members of the nightshade family, such as the eggplant, potato, and tomato, yield popular foods. Many members of the family contain alkaloids, some of which are poisonous (see ALKALOID). The belladonna plant is also called deadly nightshade. If the plant is eaten, it can cause convulsions and death. The belladonna plant contains the drug atropine which, in small amounts, is a useful

NIGHTSHADE FAMILY

The potato plant (right) is a useful member of the nightshade family. Eggplant and tomato are other edible members. But many nightshades are very poisonous to humans, including deadly nightshade or belladonna (below).

metal. For example, potassium nitrate has the H replaced by potassium (K). Its formula is KNO_3. The hydrogen can also be replaced by the ammonium group to form ammonium nitrate, NH_4NO_3. All nitrates contain the nitrate ion, NO_3^- (see IONS AND IONIZATION). Nitrates can be made by reacting nitric acid with either the metal or its oxide, hydroxide, or carbonate. Potassium, sodium, and calcium nitrates are important fertilizers. They supply plants with nitrogen. Many explosives contain nitrates. For example, potassium nitrate is used in gunpowder. Nitrates are used because they provide explosives with the oxygen they need in order to burn.

See also EXPLOSIVE; FERTILIZER; NITRIC ACID; SALT-PETER; SALTS.

medicine. Other nightshades, including bittersweet or woody nightshade, are also poisonous. Tobacco contains the alkaloid nicotine. The nightshade family also includes the mandrake.

See also TOBACCO.

NITRATE Nitrates are salts of nitric acid. The formula for nitric acid is HNO_3. Nitrates are made by replacing the hydrogen (H) in nitric acid by a

NITRIC ACID Nitric acid (HNO_3) is a colorless liquid. It is very poisonous and corrosive, and it gives off choking fumes. Nitric acid dissolves most metals to form salts called nitrates. Most nitric acid is used as nitrates for fertilizers (see CORROSION; FERTILIZER; NITRATE). Nitric acid reacts with many organic (carbon-containing) compounds to form nitro-compounds (see COMPOUND). Some nitro-compounds, such as nitroglycerin and TNT (trinitrotoluene), are explosives. Nitro-compounds are also used in making dyes (see DYE; EXPLOSIVE; TNT).

Most nitric acid is made from the gas ammonia. Ammonia and air are heated with a catalyst. The catalyst is a gauze made of an alloy of platinum and iridium. The ammonia and the oxygen in the air react together to form nitric acid. The catalyst begins the reaction and helps it go faster (see ALLOY; CATALYST). Nitric acid is formed in the air during thunderstorms. Lightning causes the oxygen and the nitrogen in the air to combine. Oxides of nitrogen are formed (see OXIDE). The oxides dissolve in the rain to form nitric acid. However, the nitric acid is very much diluted by the rainwater. *See also* ACID.

NITROGEN (nī′ trə jən) Nitrogen (N) is a colorless and odorless gaseous element (see ELEMENT; GAS). It is the most common gas in the air.

Nitrogen was discovered by the Scottish chemist Daniel Rutherford in 1772. He was the first to publish his observations about it. Other chemists in England (Joseph Priestley and Henry Cavendish) and in Sweden (Carl Wilhelm Scheele) also discovered nitrogen. A Frenchman, Antoine Lavoisier, first recognized it as an element (see CAVENDISH, HENRY; LAVOISIER, ANTOINE; PRIESTLEY, JOSEPH; SCHEELE, CARL WILHELM).

Besides nitrogen, air contains three other main gases: argon, carbon dioxide, and oxygen (see AIR).

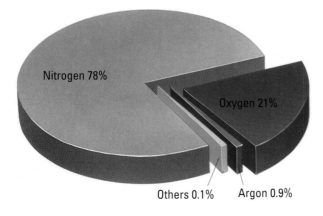

NITROGEN

Nitrogen is a chemically unreactive gas. It makes up 78 percent of the gas in air (by volume). The two other chief gases in air are oxygen (21 percent) and argon (0.9 percent). There are also small traces of carbon dioxide and other gases.

Nitrogen is obtained by cooling air until it turns into a liquid. The carbon dioxide liquefies first and is removed. The liquid air is then allowed to boil. The nitrogen boils off before the oxygen and the argon, and so the gases are separated. This process is called fractional distillation (see DISTILLATION). Most nitrogen is used for making the gas ammonia (see AMMONIA). Liquid nitrogen is used for cooling.

Nitrogen forms many different kinds of compounds (see COMPOUND). Compounds of nitrogen with one other element are called either nitrides or azides. Nitrides are very hard substances. Many azides are explosives. Many organic compounds (compounds containing carbon) contain nitrogen. The most important of these are the amines and the amino acids (see AMINE; AMINO ACID). Ammonia is an inorganic compound of nitrogen and hydrogen. Compounds containing ammonia are used as fertilizers. Other important inorganic compounds of nitrogen are nitric acid and nitrates, which are salts of nitric acid (see FERTILIZER; NITRATE; NITRIC ACID). Nitrogen combines with oxygen to form a number of oxides. These include nitrous oxide (N_2O), or laughing gas. Nitrous oxide is a colorless gas that is used as an anesthetic (see ANESTHETIC; NITROUS OXIDE). Nitric oxide (NO) is a colorless gas. It combines immediately with oxygen to form either nitrogen dioxide (NO_2) or nitrogen tetroxide (N_2O_4). Nitrogen tetroxide is a brown gas.

Nitrogen is an essential element for life. All living things contain nitrogen compounds. Some bacteria can obtain their nitrogen from the air and convert it into nitrogen compounds. This process is called nitrogen fixation (see NITROGEN FIXATION). These nitrogen compounds are then used by plants as a source of nitrogen. These plants are in turn eaten by humans and other animals. Eventually, the nitrogen compounds return to the soil. They are then absorbed again by plants. The nitrogen compounds can also be broken down, releasing the nitrogen into the air. This is called the nitrogen cycle (see NITROGEN CYCLE).

Nitrogen's atomic number is 7, and its relative atomic mass is 14.0067. Nitrogen boils at -320.4°F [-195.8°C] and freezes at -346.0°F [-210.0°C].

The nitrogen cycle (nī′ trə jən sī′ kəl) is the continuous circulation of nitrogen among the soil, water, air, and living organisms. All living organisms need nitrogen. It is part of proteins and nucleic acids, both of which are vital to life. Although almost 80 percent of the air is nitrogen, most plants and animals cannot use nitrogen in its gaseous form. The nitrogen must be "fixed"—that is, combined with other elements to form usable nitrogenous compounds (see COMPOUND; NITROGEN).

Nitrogenous compounds are formed in several ways. Some nitrogen is removed from the air and made into nitrogenous compounds by certain bacteria in a process called nitrogen fixation (see NITROGEN FIXATION). Some is removed from the air by lightning. The sudden burst of electricity causes some of the nitrogen and oxygen in the air to combine, forming nitrogen oxides. When these nitrogen oxides are dissolved in water, they can combine with other elements to form usable nitrogenous compounds.

Decaying plants and animals and decaying animal wastes release ammonia, a nitrogen-containing compound (see AMMONIA). Special bacteria, called nitrifying bacteria, convert ammonia into nitrogenous compounds that can be used by plants. Animals get their nitrogenous compounds by eating plants or other animals that eat plants. This is all part of the food chain (see FOOD CHAIN).

Although a certain amount of nitrogen is constantly being removed from the air, an approximately equal amount is being returned. Bacteria called denitrifying bacteria change some of the nitrogenous compounds in the soil back into gaseous forms of nitrogen. These gases then return to the air.

Thus, in the nitrogen cycle, nitrogen starts in the air, goes through the food chain, and returns to the air. Part of this nitrogen recycles through the food chain several times before returning to the air. A nitrogen cycle may take several years to complete.

NITROGEN CYCLE

The nitrogen cycle is a series of chemical reactions that circulate nitrogen. Plants absorb nitrogen compounds in the soil and turn them into proteins. Plant-eating animals eat these proteins, and flesh-eating animals eat the plant eaters. Bacteria return the nitrogen in animal excrement and decaying plants and animals to the soil. Lightning converts nitrogen in the air into nitrogen oxides, which also pass into the soil.

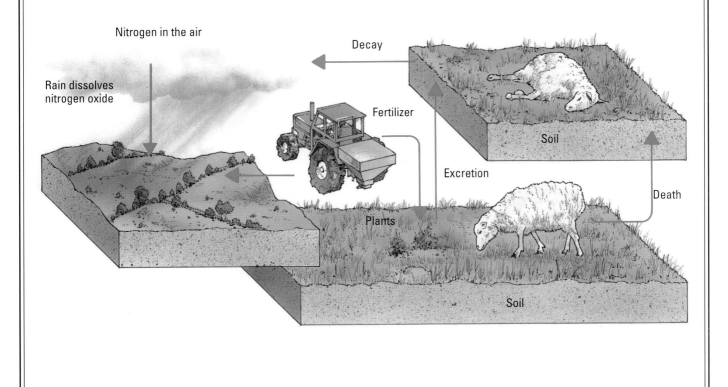

Nitrogen in the air

Rain dissolves nitrogen oxide

Decay

Fertilizer

Soil

Excretion

Death

Plants

Soil

NITROGEN FIXATION

NITROGEN FIXATION (nī′ trə jən fĭk sā′ shən) Plants can take simple substances such as water and carbon dioxide and turn them into sugar. However, they cannot make the proteins that are necessary for survival from the nitrogen in the air. Plants need to have the nitrogen in the form of compounds, such as nitrates (see COMPOUND; NITRATE). They get nitrates from the soil through their roots. Some nitrates in the soil are made by bacteria from decaying animals and plants. Other nitrates are made by bacteria that can capture nitrogen gas from the air. The process of making nitrogenous compounds from nitrogen gas is called nitrogen fixation (see BACTERIA).

Three kinds of bacteria that live in the soil and "fix" nitrogen are called *Azotobacter, Bacillus,* and *Clostridium.* Some bacteria, called *Rhizobium,* live inside plant roots, especially on the roots of certain plants of the pea family. These roots have small knobs called nodules, and these nitrogen-fixing bacteria live inside the nodules. The bacteria get food from the plant at the same time. This kind of relationship is called symbiosis. Some other plants, such as rice, have symbiotic blue-green algae, which also "fix" nitrogen.

See also ALGAE; NITROGEN; NITROGEN CYCLE; PEA FAMILY; SYMBIOSIS.

NITROUS OXIDE (nī′ trəs ŏk′ sīd′) Nitrous oxide (N_2O) is also called laughing gas. It is a colorless gas that has virtually no smell or taste. People do not really laugh when they take nitrous oxide. However, the gas causes them to feel no pain. If a person breathes in enough laughing gas, he or she may lose consciousness. This does not last long.

Nitrous oxide is a weak anesthetic (see ANESTHETIC). To be effective, a high concentration must be used. The body cannot use the oxygen in nitrous oxide, so doctors always mix oxygen with it. Dentists use nitrous oxide as a general anesthetic. Doctors often use nitrous oxide along with other anesthetics for operations. Nitrous oxide is useful for such purposes because it acts quickly and wears off quickly.

NITROGEN FIXATION
Some plants of the pea family have bacteria in their roots. An example is the soybean (right). The bacteria live in small knobs called nodules, seen here on an uprooted plant (above). The bacteria convert nitrogen gas in the soil into compounds that the plant uses for growth.

ALFRED NOBEL
Alfred Nobel is probably best known today for giving the money for the yearly Nobel Prizes. Nobel made his fortune from his invention of dynamite.

NOBEL, ALFRED (1833–1896) Alfred Nobel was a Swedish inventor. His most famous invention is dynamite. Nobel's father was also an inventor. He was very interested in explosives, particularly nitroglycerin (see EXPLOSIVE). Alfred Nobel started to manufacture nitroglycerin. However, nitroglycerin is a dangerous explosive because it is very sensitive to shocks. Many accidents occurred with nitroglycerin. One day in 1866, Nobel found that some nitroglycerin had leaked from its cask. The cask was packed in a substance called kieselguhr. Kieselguhr is an absorbent earthlike substance. Nobel found that nitroglycerin was much safer to handle in this state. If it was absorbed into kieselguhr, it would not accidentally explode from shocks. Nobel called his discovery dynamite. He

made a fortune by selling it. With his money, he started the Nobel Prizes.

These cash prizes are awarded for outstanding work in chemistry; economics; literature; physics; physiology or medicine; and in promoting peace. Each winner receives an equal share of the year's interest from Nobel's estate. Quite often, prizes have been divided between two or more winners.

NOBLE GAS *See* INERT GAS.

NOBLE METAL The noble metals are a group of metallic elements (see ELEMENT). The group is made up of the metals gold, silver, platinum, iridium, rhodium, osmium, ruthenium, and palladium. They are called noble because they are very unreactive. This means that they do not easily form compounds (see COMPOUND). All these metals are found by themselves in nature. Most other metals are found only combined with other elements in compounds. The noble metals are all very expensive, and some of them are used in jewelry.
See also GOLD; IRIDIUM; PLATINUM; SILVER.

NOCTURNAL BEHAVIOR (nŏk tûr′ nəl bĭ hāv′ yər) Many animals rest during the day and become active at night. These animals are said to have nocturnal behavior. Diurnal animals are active during the day and rest at night (see DIURNAL

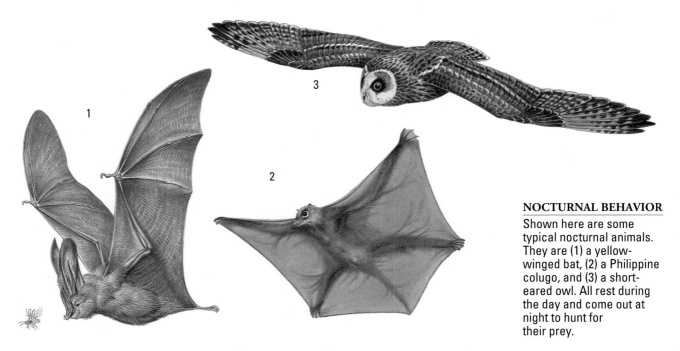

NOCTURNAL BEHAVIOR
Shown here are some typical nocturnal animals. They are (1) a yellow-winged bat, (2) a Philippine colugo, and (3) a short-eared owl. All rest during the day and come out at night to hunt for their prey.

RHYTHM). Some nocturnal animals look and act much like their diurnal relatives. Others have special adaptations to nocturnal life (see ADAPTATION). For example, owls have large eyes that can see in almost total darkness. Bats "see" in the dark by sending out high-pitched sounds. Their very sensitive ears pick up the echoes bouncing back from nearby objects and tell the bats about their surroundings (see BAT; OWL).

There are many reasons why animals have nocturnal habits. Many small animals cannot tolerate the high temperatures, bright sunshine, and dry air of the day. Predators that hunt these animals therefore have to adapt nocturnal behavior (see PREDATORS AND PREY). Some other creatures have become nocturnal as a way of avoiding diurnal predators. Nocturnal behavior seems to be instinctive (see INSTINCT).

Many plants also have nocturnal behavior. They are also called night-blooming plants. Many nocturnal plants belong to the honeysuckle and nightshade families (see HONEYSUCKLE FAMILY; NIGHTSHADE FAMILY). By blooming at night, a flower can avoid extremes of temperature and light and can be pollinated by nocturnal insects, such as the moth (see POLLINATION). These flowers are usually pale colored and highly scented to help insects find them in the darkness.

NODE In science, the term *node* has several different meanings or applications. In anatomy, a node is a knotty swelling, such as the clusters of specialized tissue that occur along lymph vessels, called lymph nodes (see LYMPHATIC SYSTEM). In botany, a node is a stem joint from which a leaf starts to grow. Corn and certain grasses are examples of plants with nodes. In astronomy, a node is one of the two points where the orbit of a planet appears to cross the ecliptic. The ecliptic is the sun's apparent path across the heavens. In geometry, a node is the point where a continuous curve crosses or meets itself. In physics, a node is the point of a vibrating object, such as a guitar string, where there is least vibration.

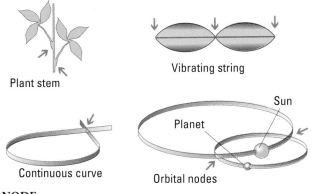

Plant stem

Vibrating string

Continuous curve

Orbital nodes

Sun

Planet

NODE

The word *node* is used with various meanings in science. Some nodes are shown here. All the arrows point to nodes.

NOISE A noise is an unwanted sound (see SOUND). The world is a noisy place, although we may not notice the noise much of the time. Our

NOISE—Ear protection
A member of the deck crew on an aircraft carrier wears ear protectors to prevent hearing damage from the noise of the helicopter's gas turbine engine. The protectors also carry headphones for a two-way radio.

NOISE—Loudness levels
With a decibel level of
more than 170 dB, a rocket
at lift-off makes one of the
loudest noises. This level
of noise is beyond the pain
threshold, and may
permanently damage
hearing.

brains are good at blocking out the sounds we do not want to hear. In scientific terms, noise is made up of an irregular pattern of sound waves. Noise does not have a single pitch or frequency like a pleasant musical sound does (see FREQUENCY).

The loudness (total energy) of a noise is measured in units called decibels (dB) (see DECIBEL). A sound of zero decibels is almost too faint to be heard by the human ear. A whisper is about 15 decibels. A vacuum cleaner produces about 70 decibels of noise. A rock band can produce 100 decibels or more of noise. Loud noises can cause deafness. People who have to work in noisy places must wear ear protectors to reduce the noise reaching their ears. Listening to loud music at a rock concert, or through headphones, can cause hearing loss.   PROJECT 47

NONRENEWABLE RESOURCES Non-
renewable resources are natural resources that cannot be replaced at all or within a reasonable time (see NATURAL RESOURCES). Fossil fuels such as oil,

gas, and coal are examples of nonrenewable resources (see COAL; FOSSIL FUEL; GAS; OIL). These resources accumulated over millions of years. They are considered to be nonrenewable resources because once they are used up, they are gone forever. Scientists estimate that there are enough deposits of fossil fuel resources to last for only one or two centuries before supplies run out. In contrast, energy sources such as nuclear power from hydrogen fusion, and solar, wind, and wave energy are considered to be renewable resources because people expect that hydrogen (from water), sun, wind, and waves will always be available.   PROJECT 70

NORMAL SOLUTION A normal solution is
one that contains one gram-equivalent of a substance in a liter of the solution (see EQUIVALENT; SOLUTION AND SOLUBILITY). The gram-equivalent of a substance is the number of grams that will combine with or displace one gram of hydrogen or eight grams of oxygen. The concept of normality

is most often applied to solutions of acids and bases (see ACID; BASE). For example, nitric acid (HNO_3) has a molecular mass of 63 (see RELATIVE MOLECULAR MASS). Its molecules each contain one hydrogen atom. Therefore, its gram equivalent is 63 g [2.3 oz.]. Sulfuric acid (H_2SO_4) has a relative molecular mass of 98. However, it has two hydrogen atoms in each molecule. Therefore, its gram equivalent is 98 divided by 2, or 49 g [1.8 oz.]. A normal solution of nitric acid contains 63 g [2.3 oz.] of nitric acid in a liter. A normal solution of sulfuric acid contains 49 g [1.8 oz.] of sulfuric acid in a liter. Normal solutions of two different acids contain the same amount of hydrogen. Today, molar solutions are usually used instead of normal solutions.

See also MOLE (UNIT).

NORTH STAR The North Star, also called Polaris, is a star located one degree from the north celestial pole (see CELESTIAL SPHERE). Because of its location, the North Star is an important aid to navigators. The altitude of the North Star above the horizon is roughly equal to the observer's latitude north of the equator (see ALTITUDE; LATITUDE AND LONGITUDE). The North Star is the brightest star of

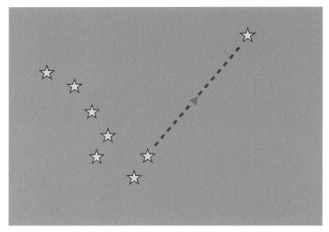

NORTH STAR
The North Star can be located in the night sky by extending a line joining the two end stars of the constellation called the Big Dipper (Ursa Major). For this reason, the two stars are known as the pointers.

the constellation Ursa Minor. However, it is only the fiftieth brightest star in the sky.

See also CONSTELLATION; NAVIGATION; STAR.

NOSE The nose is an organ used for smelling and breathing (see BREATHING; TASTE AND SMELL). During breathing, air enters the nose through two openings called nostrils. The nostrils are separated by a thin wall of cartilage (tough tissue) and bone, called the septum. Air passes from the nostrils

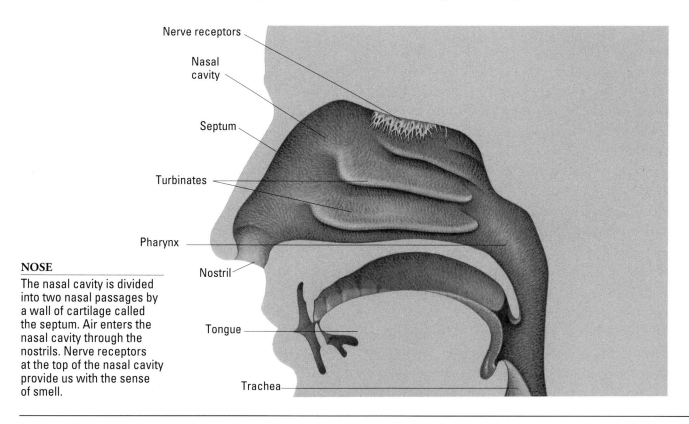

Nerve receptors
Nasal cavity
Septum
Turbinates
Pharynx
Nostril
Tongue
Trachea

NOSE
The nasal cavity is divided into two nasal passages by a wall of cartilage called the septum. Air enters the nasal cavity through the nostrils. Nerve receptors at the top of the nasal cavity provide us with the sense of smell.

into the nasal cavity, which leads back to the upper part of the throat. Air then passes through a cavity called the pharynx and the trachea (windpipe) into the lungs.

The nasal passages are lined with mucous membrane. The mucous membrane is covered with tiny, hairlike projections called cilia (see CILIUM; MUCOUS MEMBRANE). The cilia wave back and forth constantly, moving dust, microorganisms, and fluids from the nose to the throat for swallowing (see MICROORGANISM). Large bones in the nasal passages, called turbinates, help warm the air and make it more moist before it enters the lungs.

The sense of smell is due to olfactory nerve receptors. These receptors lie in mucous membrane in the highest part of the nose. Chemicals in the air cause the receptors to send out impulses. Olfactory nerve fibers carry these impulses to the brain (see BRAIN; NERVOUS SYSTEM; RECEPTOR).

The sense of smell is closely related to the sense of taste. Some foods would not taste as they do if a person could not smell them while eating them. For example, apples and potatoes can be smelled as they are eaten. However, if a person could not use his or her senses of sight and smell along with taste, it would be difficult to tell apples and potatoes apart when eating them.

Colds often hamper the sense of smell. This happens because the cold infection thickens the mucous membrane of the nasal passages. This prevents air from reaching the olfactory nerve receptors.

See also COLD, COMMON; INFECTION.

PROJECT 63, 74

NOTOCHORD (nō′ tə kôrd′) The notochord is the hard but bendable rod of cartilage (tough tissue) that extends along the bodies of all chordates at some stage in their lives. In the vertebrates, including humans, the notochord exists only in the embryo. It is replaced by the spine, or backbone, as the animal develops. However, in primitive chordates, such as the amphioxus, the notochord remains in the adult (see CARTILAGE; CHORDATA; VERTEBRATE).

Biologists believe that the notochord's main

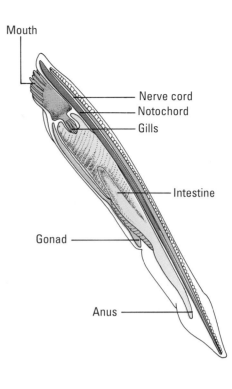

NOTOCHORD

The amphioxus, shown in cross section, is a primitive aquatic animal that has a notochord throughout its life. Animals with backbones have a notochord only during the embryo stage.

function is to anchor the organism's body muscles so that it can swim with S-shaped movements. With a stiff rod to pull against, this muscular action is much more efficient than it is in soft-bodied animals.

NOVA A nova is a star that suddenly increases in brightness. This happens when a star larger than the sun explodes, throwing off up to 10 percent of its matter. An exploding nova may become 100,000 times brighter than the original star. It may take a few hours or a few days for a nova to reach its maximum brilliance before it fades gradually back to its normal brightness. Novae (plural of *nova*) occur in binary (two-star) systems in which one star is a white dwarf (see DWARF STAR). Material falls onto the white dwarf and explodes when it hits either the surface of the white dwarf or the disk of material around it. The total energy released on the explosion is the same as would be released by 1,000 million million nuclear bombs, or as much energy as the sun emits in 10,000 years.

A recurrent nova is a nova that has had more than one observed massive explosion. All novae are probably recurrent. However, they only flare up at long intervals. About two novae per year are observed in the Milky Way galaxy. Other galaxies have a similar rate of nova occurrence (see GALAXY).

A supernova is a much more spectacular event than a nova (see SUPERNOVA). A supernova occurs when a star larger than the sun throws off more than 10 percent of its matter in an explosion. A supernova may be 1,000 times brighter than a nova. In the year 1054, a supernova was observed that was bright enough to be seen during the day. The remains of this explosion make up the Crab Nebula.

See also NEBULA; STAR.

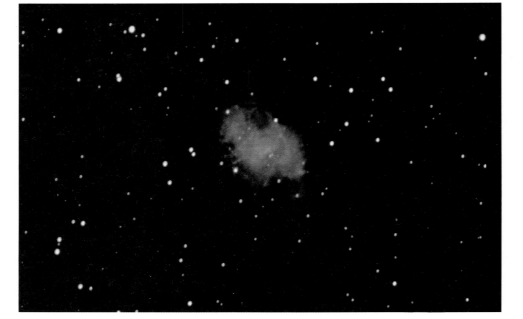

NOVA

The Crab Nebula (left) is a huge mass of dust and gas. It was formed when a supernova exploded. The stages leading up to a nova are shown below. They are (1) a binary star system, (2) the formation of a red giant, (3) a red giant becomes a white dwarf, (4) the small star grows into a red giant, (5) matter transfers to a white dwarf, (6) matter becomes compressed, (7) nuclear fusion begins, and (8) the nova explodes.

NUCLEAR ENERGY

Nuclear energy (noo' klē ər ĕn' ər jē) is one of the newest forms of energy (see ENERGY). People are using more energy today than ever before. Most of this energy is supplied by fossil fuels, such as coal, gas, and oil (see FOSSIL FUEL). However, there is only a certain amount of these fuels in the earth. Once they are used up, new sources of energy will be needed. In addition, the burning of fossil fuels releases large amounts of pollutants into the atmosphere (see POLLUTION). Some experts think that the best new source of energy is nuclear energy from radioactive elements such as uranium. These elements are called nuclear fuels. Nuclear fuels are rare and expensive. However, a piece of uranium weighing just 1 lb. [0.45 kg] produces more energy than 1,100 tons [1,000 metric tons] of coal.

Nuclear energy is obtained by splitting the nuclei (plural of *nucleus*) of radioactive atoms (see ATOM; RADIOACTIVITY). A radioactive atom is unstable. It can be split in a process called fission (see FISSION). Fission is carried out in devices called nuclear reactors. The energy made in a nuclear reactor can be changed into electrical energy. The world's first nuclear reactor was built in 1942 at the University of Chicago. It was built by a team of scientists led by the Italian physicist Enrico Fermi (see FERMI, ENRICO). Today, many countries have nuclear reactors to supply them with energy. Nuclear reactors are also used to drive ships and submarines. The *Nautilus* was the first nuclear-powered submarine. It was launched by the United States in 1954. The first nuclear-powered ship, the American merchant ship *Savannah,* was launched in 1959. Spacecraft may someday be nuclear powered.

Nuclear energy has both advantages and disadvantages. Nuclear reactors provide large amounts of energy. However, nuclear reactors also produce radioactive waste that has to be disposed of. At present, the waste is put into radiation-proof containers. These containers are then stored at the nuclear power plant. There is no permanent way to dispose of these wastes (see WASTE DISPOSAL). Scientists are researching ways to convert or reprocess radioactive wastes into less harmful substances that can be reused or disposed of more easily. The large amounts of energy produced by nuclear reactions is also a disadvantage. When fission occurs in a nuclear reactor, it is controlled. However, there is always a slight chance that a nuclear reactor might lose control. Very high standards of safety are needed in the nuclear power plants that house nuclear reactors. Another disadvantage of nuclear power plants is that they are very costly to build. Some people argue against building more nuclear

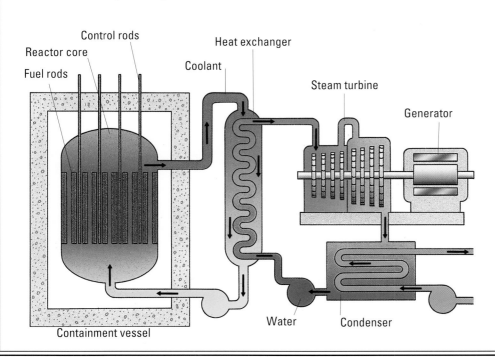

NUCLEAR POWER PLANT

In a nuclear power station, the reactor heats water to make steam. The steam spins a turbine which, in turn, turns a generator to produce electricity. Waste steam is condensed back to water and recycled.

Control rods
Reactor core
Fuel rods
Heat exchanger
Coolant
Steam turbine
Generator
Water
Condenser
Containment vessel

reactors. They think that other sources of energy, such as solar energy, should be used as well or instead.

Nuclear reactions Fission is an example of a nuclear reaction. Fission occurs when the nuclei of radioactive atoms are struck by subatomic particles and split in two (see NUCLEUS). Subatomic particles include those particles, such as electrons, neutrons, and protons, that are smaller than the atom. As fission occurs, a small amount of the mass of the atoms is converted to huge amounts of energy (see MASS). Albert Einstein was the first to explain that mass and energy are different aspects of the same thing, in his theory of relativity (see EINSTEIN, ALBERT; RELATIVITY). Neutrons may also be released. These neutrons can collide with other nuclei and split them, releasing still more energy. This is called a chain reaction (see CHAIN REACTION). It occurs when there is more than a certain amount of the radioactive material. This amount is called the critical mass. If the mass of the radioactive material is less than the critical mass, some of the neutrons can escape from the material. Therefore, they do not split any other nuclei, and the reaction slows down. If the mass is greater than the critical mass, then not many neutrons escape. Enough neutrons collide with nuclei to keep the reaction going. If the reaction is uncontrolled, such as in an atomic bomb, an explosion follows (see NUCLEAR WEAPONS). If the reaction is controlled, such as in a nuclear reactor, it can provide a steady supply of heat.

How nuclear reactors work Nuclear reactors are large structures made of thick concrete and steel. The most important part of a nuclear reactor is called the core. The core contains the nuclear fuel. The fuel can be either a solid or a liquid. The fuel is surrounded by a coolant. The coolant is either a liquid or a gas, and often it is water. Fission of the fuel heats up the coolant. The hot coolant is pumped into a heat exchanger. The heat exchanger contains water circulating in pipes. The coolant heats up the water in the pipes and converts it into steam. The steam is then used to drive a turbine

(see TURBINE). The turbine, in turn, drives a generator to generate electricity (see ELECTRICITY; GENERATOR, ELECTRICAL). In this way, heat from the fission of the fuel is converted into electricity.

Most reactors use uranium as a fuel (see URANIUM). The uranium used is a mixture of two forms called isotopes. All uranium atoms contain ninety-two protons in the nucleus. However, the number of neutrons in the nucleus can vary. Atoms of the same element, but with different numbers of neutrons, are called isotopes (see ISOTOPE). The two main isotopes in uranium fuel are uranium-235 and uranium-238. Their names are usually shortened to U-235 and U-238. The U-235 nuclei split much more easily than the U-238 nuclei. However, the amount of U-235 in natural uranium is very small, and isotopes are difficult to separate. The neutrons given off by U-235 nuclei are called fast neutrons because they move at very high speeds. To start a chain reaction, they must hit another U-235 nucleus and not a U-238 nucleus. Because of their speed, however, fast neutrons often escape from the fuel. Also, fast neutrons are easily absorbed by U-238 nuclei. Therefore, the neutrons have to be slowed down. Slow neutrons are less likely to escape and are not absorbed by U-238 nuclei. The neutrons are slowed down by devices called moderator rods. Moderators are usually made out of graphite, beryllium, or heavy water (see MODERATOR).

Uranium
mine

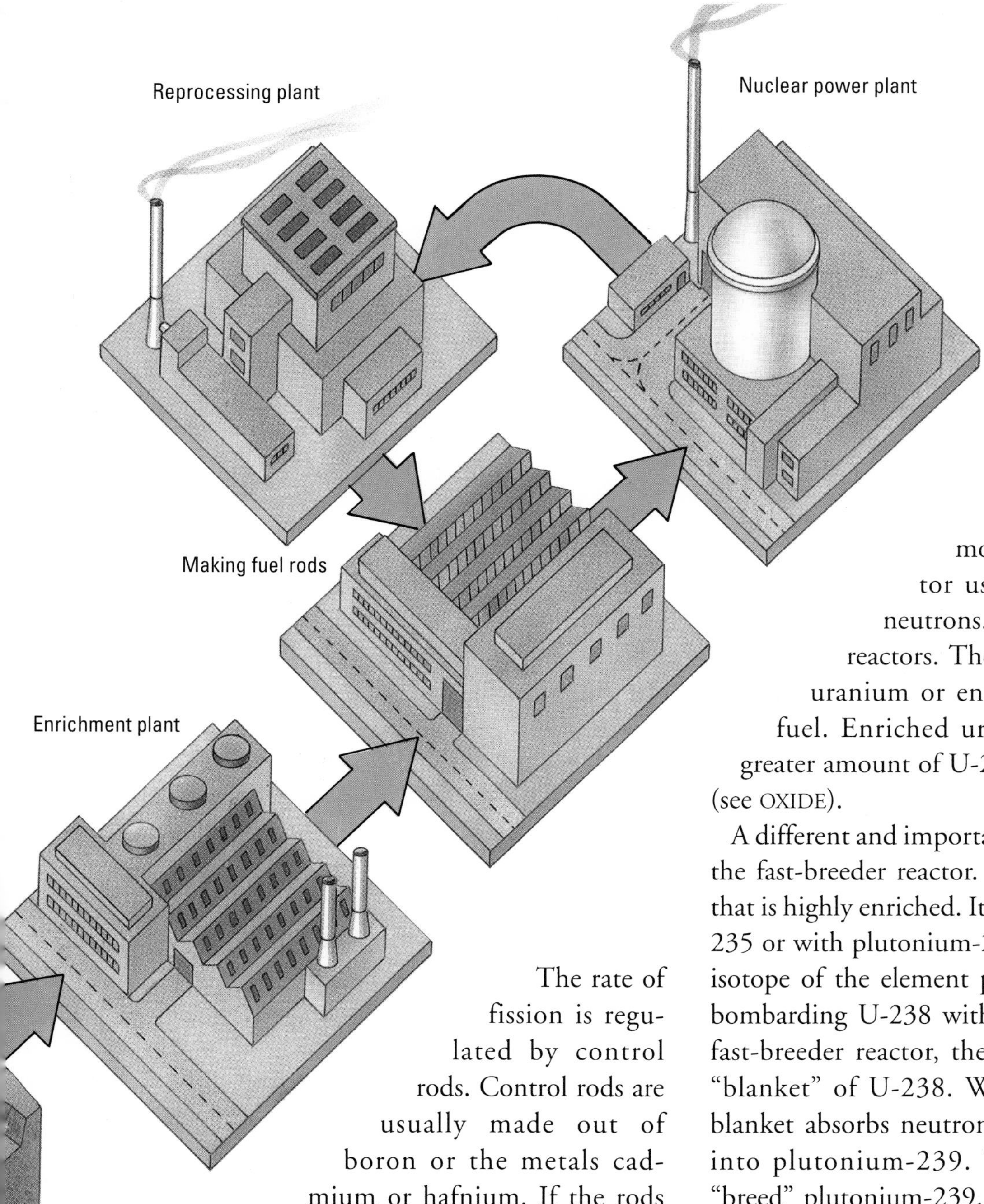

Reprocessing plant

Nuclear power plant

URANIUM CYCLE

Uranium is extracted from ore from a mine and enriched (its U-235 content increased) before being made into fuel rods. The fuel rods "power" the reactor. Old fuel rods are reprocessed to produce more fuel.

Making fuel rods

Enrichment plant

Types of reactors The most common type of reactor uses moderators and slow neutrons. They are called thermal reactors. Thermal reactors use natural uranium or enriched uranium oxide as fuel. Enriched uranium oxide contains a greater amount of U-235 than normal uranium (see OXIDE).

A different and important type of reactor is called the fast-breeder reactor. Its fuel is uranium oxide that is highly enriched. It is enriched either with U-235 or with plutonium-239. Plutonium-239 is an isotope of the element plutonium. It is made by bombarding U-238 with very fast neutrons. In a fast-breeder reactor, the fuel is surrounded by a "blanket" of U-238. When fission occurs, this blanket absorbs neutrons. This turns the U-238 into plutonium-239. The reaction is said to "breed" plutonium-239. The plutonium-239 that is produced can be extracted and used to enrich the fuel. The fast-breeder reactor needs no moderator. Therefore, it is smaller than the thermal reactor. It uses liquid sodium as a coolant. However, there are doubts about the safety of the fast-breeder reactor. Plutonium is a very dangerous substance (see PLUTONIUM).

The rate of fission is regulated by control rods. Control rods are usually made out of boron or the metals cadmium or hafnium. If the rods are lowered into the core of nuclear fuel, they slow down the reaction by absorbing neutrons. The reaction is speeded up by withdrawing the control rods.

The fission process produces dangerous radiation, as well as heat (see RADIATION). The core is shielded with thick concrete to keep the radiation in. This protects the workers at the plant. The concrete is lined with steel as an extra safety measure. These measures also guard against the core burning through the structure that contains it.

Thermonuclear power A very different kind of nuclear energy is called thermonuclear energy. Thermonuclear energy involves the process of nuclear fusion (see FUSION). In fusion, two nuclei

REACTOR CORE
The core of a nuclear reactor at Rainier, Oregon, can be seen in the center of this picture. The core is under 35 ft. [11 m] of water. The heat from the reactor produces superheated steam in the four steam generators on each side of the core. The steam then passes to steam turbines, which spin generators to produce electricity.

are joined together—rather than split apart as they are in fission—to form one nucleus. Fusion also produces large amounts of energy. For example, two deuterium nuclei can be joined together. They may form the nucleus of a helium atom and an extra neutron. The new nucleus weighs less than the two original nuclei. The missing mass has been converted to energy. Uncontrolled fusion takes place in hydrogen bombs. It is also responsible for the heat and light of the sun. To start nuclear fusion, temperatures of over a million degrees Fahrenheit are needed. That is why the reaction is called thermonuclear. Scientists have not yet been able to reach these high temperatures for any length of time. Another problem is controlling the reaction. If these problems could be solved, the world's energy problems might also be solved. There are vast amounts of deuterium in ordinary seawater that would provide an almost unlimited amount of energy. In addition, production of thermonuclear energy produces little waste. This makes thermonuclear energy a possible alternative to fission and fossil fuels.

Nuclear reactor accidents Because a nuclear reactor produces such a large amount of radiation, any mechanical failures or human errors can have disastrous results. For example, in 1986, an accident occurred at a nuclear power plant in Chernobyl, a city in Ukraine (see CHERNOBYL). The accident is believed to have been caused by errors in how the cooling system was used, so that the cooling system did not operate properly. The system failed to cool the core, and temperatures quickly soared inside the reactor. A fire and explosions resulted, and dangerous amounts of radiation were released. The accident killed 7 firefighters and 24 plant workers. About 100,000 people from Chernobyl and neighboring communities had to be evacuated for a long period of time. Many had severe cases of radiation sickness. Radiation sickness generally lasts about two weeks. However, in severe cases, the skin is burned. The body's ability to fight infection is also affected, and death may result. In addition, the land around Chernobyl can no longer be farmed. The long-term effects of the accident may not be known for many years.

A similar accident occurred in 1979 at the Three Mile Island nuclear power plant near Harrisburg, Pennsylvania. At Three Mile Island, both human error and mechanical failure caused the cooling system to fail. The core became so hot that it started to melt. However, workers corrected the problem before the core could melt completely and burn through the structure that contained it. Only a small amount of radiation was released. Workers and neighboring communities were evacuated for a short time.

NUCLEAR MEDICINE (nŏŏ′ klē ər mĕd′ ĭ sĭn)

Nuclear medicine is a branch of medicine that diagnoses disease by using substances that have been made radioactive (see RADIATION; RADIOACTIVITY). Nuclear medicine procedures are effective in showing how well the heart, kidneys, liver, gallbladder, and other organs are working. The nuclear medicine procedure called a bone scan is an accurate way to evaluate a patient's bones to see if there is cancer, infection, or injury to them.

In a typical nuclear medicine procedure, a patient is given a small amount of a radioactive substance. The type of substance given depends on what organ or other internal structure is to be studied. The substance may be injected into a patient's vein, swallowed, or inhaled.

Certain substances that have been made radioactive are attracted to certain organs. For example, a proteinlike substance that has been made radioactive settles primarily in the lungs. This substance can be used to diagnose blood clots in the lungs.

In most studies, the patient lies on a table. A large instrument called a scintillation camera is positioned over the area to be studied. As the radioactive substance breaks down within the body, it gives off gamma rays (see GAMMA RAY). The camera senses the radioactive substance in the organ, tissue, or bone being studied. The camera records this information on a display screen or on film to be later studied by a specially trained physician.

In some nuclear medicine studies, a urine or stool sample is taken. The amount of radioactivity in the sample shows how certain parts of the body, such as the kidneys or intestines, are working.

Only a small amount of radiation is used in nuclear medicine studies. The amount of radiation is carefully selected to provide the least amount of radiation exposure while still allowing for an accurate examination.

See also RADIOLOGY.

NUCLEAR PHYSICS (nŏŏ′ klē ər fĭz′ ĭks)

Nuclear physics is the study of the atomic nucleus. Every atom has a nucleus at its center. The nucleus contains most of the mass of the atom (see ATOM; MASS; NUCLEUS). The nuclei of all elements except one contain particles called protons and neutrons. (The one exception is ordinary hydrogen, which has only a proton.) Some nuclei, especially the larger ones, are unstable. They disintegrate and give off particles. The nucleus is then said to be radioactive (see RADIOACTIVITY). An important part of nuclear physics is the study of radioactive nuclei.

Nuclear physicists use a machine called a particle accelerator (see ACCELERATORS, PARTICLE). In a particle accelerator, beams of subatomic particles are made to collide with nuclei. Subatomic particles include those particles, such as the electron, neutron, and proton, that are smaller than the atom. These collisions sometimes cause the nuclei to break up. Other times, the nuclei absorb the particles and become different nuclei. Many new elements have been made in this way.

See also ELEMENT.

NUCLEAR WEAPONS (nŏŏ′ klē ər wĕp′ ənz)

Nuclear weapons are the most deadly weapons that have ever been used. The first nuclear weapons to be built were fission weapons such as the atomic bomb, or A-bomb. The A-bomb was first built in the United States during World War II (1939–1945). Two A-bombs were dropped on the Japanese cities of Hiroshima and Nagasaki. The explosive force of a nuclear weapon is measured in metric tons of TNT. The force of the bombs dropped on Hiroshima was equivalent to 12,000 metric tons of TNT (see TNT).

During the 1950s, the first thermonuclear weapon, the hydrogen bomb, or H-bomb, was developed. The H-bomb is much more powerful than the A-bomb. Some H-bombs are equivalent to hundreds of millions of metric tons of TNT. The blast from an H-bomb can destroy an area of 200 sq. mi. [500 sq. km]. The fire caused by an H-bomb can destroy an even greater area of about 1,000 sq. mi. [3,000 sq. km].

The nuclei of certain atoms can be split in two. This is called fission (see FISSION). When the nucleus splits, it sometimes gives off small particles called neutrons (see NEUTRON). These neutrons can collide with other nuclei and cause them to split.

NUCLEAR WEAPONS
The nuclear installation at the Oak Ridge National Laboratory in Tennessee (shown here) dates back to 1943, when it was set up to produce the uranium for the world's first atomic bomb.

This series of reactions is called a chain reaction (see CHAIN REACTION). In this way, the reaction can spread throughout the whole of the substance. This happens when the mass of the substance is greater than a certain mass called the critical mass (see MASS). If the mass is below the critical mass, the reaction dies away. In an A-bomb, the substance used is usually either of the isotopes uranium-235 or plutonium-239. They are both radioactive (see ISOTOPE; PLUTONIUM; RADIOACTIVITY; URANIUM). An A-bomb contains two pieces of the substance. On their own, they are stable because their masses are less than the critical mass. If they are brought together, their total mass becomes greater than the critical mass. A nuclear reaction takes place. Some of the mass of the nuclei is converted into energy. The energy appears as light and heat and also as the explosive blast of the bomb. The nuclear reaction gives off large amounts of radioactive products. These products are scattered over a very wide area and cause great damage.

The energy in an H-bomb is produced by fusion of deuterium and tritium. Deuterium and tritium are isotopes of hydrogen (see FUSION). In fusion, the nuclei of deuterium and tritium fuse (join) together to form one nucleus. Fusion reactions give out much more energy than fission reactions. This makes the H-bomb much more powerful than the A-bomb. The nuclei can only fuse together at very high temperatures. Therefore, large amounts of heat are needed to set the reaction going. This heat is provided by an A-bomb. Thus, an H-bomb weapon contains an A-bomb to act as a trigger.
See also NUCLEAR ENERGY.

NUCLEIC ACID (noo klē′ ĭk ăs′ĭd) Nucleic acids are complex chemical compounds that control important cell functions. Nucleic acids are made of chains of units called nucleotides (see CELL; COMPOUND). Each nucleotide contains phosphate (a salt of phosphoric acid), a sugar, and compounds called bases (see BASE). In DNA (deoxyribonucleic acid), the sugar is deoxyribose, and the four possible bases are adenine, guanine, cytosine, and thymine. In RNA (ribonucleic acid), the sugar is ribose, and the four possible bases are adenine, guanine, cytosine, and uracil (see DNA; RNA).

DNA is composed of two nucleotide chains coiled together. This type of structure is called a double helix, and it resembles a twisted ladder. Each "rung" consists of two bases. Adenine and thymine always link together. Cytosine and guanine always link together. When a cell divides, the DNA double helix splits, and each nucleotide chain builds a new double helix, maintaining the same base pairs.

DNA plays a critical role in genetics. RNA controls the manufacture of proteins in the cells. Proteins are necessary for the survival of every living organism.
See also GENETICS; PROTEIN.

Nucleus (no͞o′ klē əs) has two different meanings in science. In biology, the nucleus is the control center of a cell (see CELL). In physics, the nucleus is the central part, or core, of an atom (see ATOM).

Nearly all plant and animal cells have a nucleus. The nucleus is bound by the nuclear membrane, and it is full of extremely small structures called chromosomes, each of which consists of DNA. The nucleus carries out its activities through the DNA, which determines what proteins are made in the cell (see DNA; RNA). A nucleus exists in almost all living cells except red blood cells and those of bacteria and certain algae, in which the DNA is scattered through the cell.

In an atom, nearly all of the mass is in the nucleus. The nucleus consists of protons and neutrons, except for the nucleus of ordinary hydrogen, which is only a proton (see NEUTRON; PROTON).

Because a proton has a positive electrical charge, the nucleus is positively charged. The nucleus is surrounded by electrons (see ELECTRON). Each electron has a negative charge equal to the positive charge of a proton. There are the same number of electrons and protons in each atom, so an atom is electrically neutral.

All the atoms of a particular chemical element have the same number of protons (see ELEMENT). But in most elements, some atoms have different numbers of neutrons. The atoms of an element that have different numbers of neutrons in the nucleus

CELL NUCLEUS

Various parts of an animal cell are shown here. All of the cell's activities are controlled by the nucleus, which has a central nucleolus and is surrounded by a nuclear membrane. The nucleus also contains the cell's chromosomes.

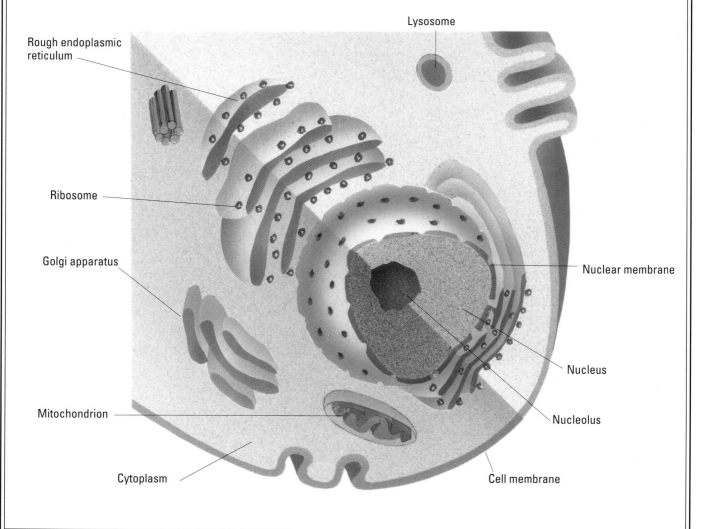

Lysosome

Rough endoplasmic reticulum

Ribosome

Golgi apparatus

Mitochondrion

Cytoplasm

Nuclear membrane

Nucleus

Nucleolus

Cell membrane

are the atoms of the isotopes of that element (see ISOTOPE).

Ernest Rutherford, a British physicist, is usually credited with discovering the nucleus because of an experiment he suggested and later explained (see RUTHERFORD, ERNEST). In the experiment, alpha particles were fired at a very thin piece of gold. Alpha particles are tiny particles given off by certain radioactive substances (see ALPHA PARTICLE; RADIOACTIVITY). Most of the alpha particles went straight through the gold. However, a few of them were deflected (turned aside), some at very large angles. Because so many of the alpha particles had been able to go straight through the gold, Rutherford concluded that most of an atom is empty space. He also suggested that atoms must have a small, heavy, positively charged core. This would explain why some of the alpha particles had

been deflected. If the core had a positive charge, it would repel (push away) alpha particles, which also have a positive charge.

In the early 1900s, Rutherford showed that the nucleus of a hydrogen atom contains just one particle. He called this particle a proton. At first, physicists thought that nuclei (plural of *nucleus*) contain only protons. For example, oxygen nuclei are about sixteen times as heavy as a proton. Therefore, physicists thought that the oxygen nuclei contained sixteen protons. However, there was a problem with this idea. Electrons, the particles that orbit the nucleus, have a negative charge. An oxygen atom contains eight electrons. If its nuclei contained sixteen protons, as physicists thought, then oxygen atoms would have a positive electric charge. However, they do not have any charge. This caused James Chadwick to predict the

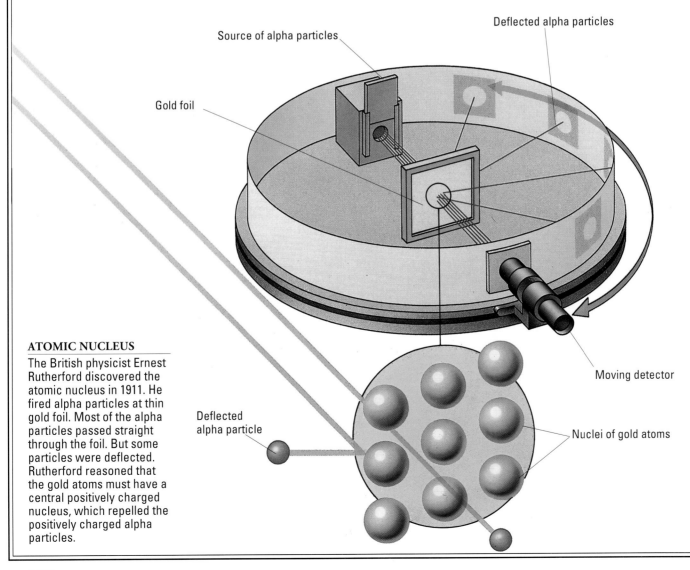

Source of alpha particles

Deflected alpha particles

Gold foil

Moving detector

Deflected alpha particle

Nuclei of gold atoms

ATOMIC NUCLEUS

The British physicist Ernest Rutherford discovered the atomic nucleus in 1911. He fired alpha particles at thin gold foil. Most of the alpha particles passed straight through the foil. But some particles were deflected. Rutherford reasoned that the gold atoms must have a central positively charged nucleus, which repelled the positively charged alpha particles.

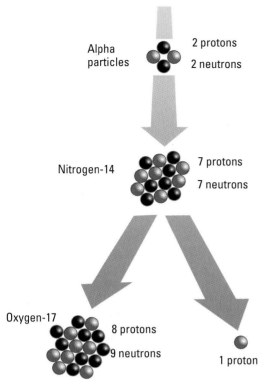

Alpha particles — 2 protons, 2 neutrons

Nitrogen-14 — 7 protons, 7 neutrons

Oxygen-17 — 8 protons, 9 neutrons

1 proton

MAKING NEW ELEMENTS

Different elements have different numbers of protons in their nuclei. In 1920, Ernest Rutherford became the first scientist to make one element into a different element. He bombarded nuclei of nitrogen with alpha particles. Some of the nitrogen nuclei were converted into nuclei of an isotope of oxygen.

existence of the neutron (see CHADWICK, SIR JAMES). Oxygen has only eight protons. The other eight particles in the oxygen nuclei are neutrons. They are slightly heavier than a proton and have no electric charge.

There was another problem to be solved about the nucleus. Charges that are alike repel each other. Therefore, the protons in a nucleus should repel each other. This would make the nucleus split apart. In fact, most nuclei are very stable. Therefore, the nucleus must be held together by a very strong force. Physicists named this force the strong nuclear force (see FORCE). The strong nuclear force is caused by tiny particles called gluons (see PARTICLE PHYSICS).

Atoms of a particular element always have the same number of protons in their nuclei. For example, oxygen nuclei always have eight protons. However, as we have seen, the number of neutrons can vary. Atoms that have the same number of protons but different numbers of neutrons are

called isotopes. For example, isotopes of oxygen can have seven, eight, nine, or ten neutrons in their nuclei. Because oxygen always has eight protons, these isotopes can have fifteen, sixteen, seventeen, or eighteen protons and neutrons altogether. They are written as oxygen-15, oxygen-16, oxygen-17, and so on.

In lighter nuclei, the number of neutrons is about the same as the number of protons. In heavier nuclei, there are more neutrons than protons. For example, lead nuclei have 82 protons and, usually, 126 neutrons. The more neutrons a nucleus has, the farther apart the protons are. This helps make the heavy nucleus, which would have a tendency to be unstable, more stable.

A radioactive element is one that has an unstable nucleus. Its nuclei decay and give off alpha particles, beta particles, or gamma rays. Alpha particles are made up of two neutrons and two protons bound together. Beta particles are electrons. Gamma rays are high-energy electromagnetic rays that are similar to X rays (see BETA PARTICLE; GAMMA RAY). Both stable and unstable nuclei can be broken down by bombarding them with subatomic particles. Subatomic particles are those particles, such as the electron, neutron, and proton, that are smaller than the atom. This was first done by Rutherford in 1919. He bombarded nitrogen-14 atoms with alpha particles. The nitrogen-14 atoms contain seven protons and seven neutrons. In Rutherford's bombardment, the nitrogen nuclei absorbed the alpha particles and gave off a proton. Therefore, the nitrogen nuclei each gained one proton and two neutrons, for a total of eight protons and nine neutrons. Because they now had eight protons, they were oxygen nuclei. One element had been changed into another. This process is called transmutation. Many new and completely artificial elements have been made in this way (see TRANSMUTATION OF ELEMENTS).

When radioactive elements, such as uranium, decay, they usually change into other radioactive elements. These elements then decay into other elements. The process continues until a stable element is reached. This is very often lead-208.

See also PERIODIC TABLE, VOL. 23.

NUMBER Whenever a person has an idea of how many objects there are in a group, such as how many coins he or she has in a pocket, that idea is called a number. Numbers are the basis of arithmetic (see ARITHMETIC).

A numeral is a written sign used to stand for a number (see NUMERAL). Counting means arranging numerals in a certain order. The numbers used for counting, such as 1, 2, 3, which are shown by Hindu-Arabic numerals, are called natural numbers. When two natural numbers are added or multiplied together, the result is another natural number.

Numbers can be shown by an order of points along a number line. Addition is performed by moving to the right. For example, 2 + 3 = 5.

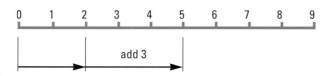

Subtracting one natural number from another natural number involves moving to the left on the number line. Sometimes, this gives another natural number. For example, 5 - 2 = 3.

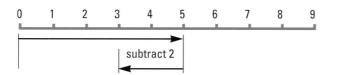

However, if 5 is subtracted from 2, there are no natural numbers left on the number line to represent the answer. For example, 2 - 5 = ?.

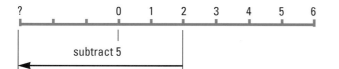

In order to subtract any two natural numbers and get a result, the system of natural numbers must be enlarged. To do this, the points left of zero are marked -1, -2, -3, and so on. This enlarged system is called the system of integers. An integer is any whole number. Positive integers are written as +1, +2, +3, or simply as 1, 2, 3, and so on. Negative integers are written as -1, -2, -3, and so on.

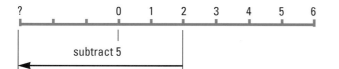

Adding a negative integer is the same as subtracting the corresponding positive integer. For example: 7 + (-3) = 7 - 3 = 4.

When two integers are multiplied together, the result is an integer. For example: 2 x 3 = 6. However, what can 2 be multiplied by to give the answer 5? There is no answer within the set of integers. To answer this question, the spaces between the integers must be filled in by inventing some new numbers. This enlarged system is called the system of rational numbers. Rational numbers are numbers that can be written as fractions, such as $^1/_2$ and $^1/_4$. They include the integers in the form $^2/_1$, $^{-5}/_1$, and so on (see ROOT, MATHEMATICAL). In the set of rational numbers, division by any number other than zero is possible.

Some numbers cannot be written as fractions. They are called irrational numbers. The irrational numbers include all the square roots that do not result in a repeating or terminating decimal, such as $\sqrt{2}$, $\sqrt{3}$, and so on. A repeating decimal is one that has a recurring number or series of numbers. A terminating decimal is one in which the division comes out even and stops. The number π (pi) is irrational, and so are most of the values of cosines, sines, and tangents (see TRIGONOMETRY). The rationals and irrationals together make up the system called real numbers. In turn, real numbers are part of a still-larger system that includes complex numbers.

See also MATHEMATICS.

NUMERAL A numeral is a written sign used to stand for a number (see NUMBER). For example, the word *seven* or the symbol 7 is used to stand for the number of days in a week. Both *seven* and 7 are numerals. Numerals are as necessary to civilization as writing. Without numerals, there could be no mathematics and therefore, no science.

In ancient times, people developed systems of numerals to allow them to do the calculations needed to make calendars, measure land, and figure taxes. For example, the ancient Babylonians of Mesopotamia (now Iraq) wrote cuneiform (wedge-shaped) numerals on clay tablets. Numbers from one to nine were shown as downward wedges, and ten was shown as a sideways wedge. To show larger numbers, the Babylonians used a multiplication system. For example, twenty was shown by two downward wedges and one sideways wedge, which meant 2 x 10.

The ancient Egyptians used curved strokes for one to nine. Tens, hundreds, and so on were shown by pictures called hieroglyphs. In this system, symbols were repeated to show twenty, thirty, and so on, rather than multiplied as in the Babylonian system.

The ancient Greeks and Romans used letters of their alphabets for numerals. This made calculations quite complicated.

The most important step in the development of numeral systems was the introduction of a zero symbol (0). This idea probably began in India and was borrowed by the Arabs, whose system is widely used today. By using one or more zeros, a single set of symbols for the numbers from one to nine can show units (ones), tens, hundreds, thousands, and so on by their position. This is called place value. For example, 4,305 means four thousands, three hundreds, no tens, and five units. By using place value, the Arabic system simplifies calculations involving large numbers.

See also ARITHMETIC; BINARY NUMBERS; MATHEMATICS.

NUT In botany, a nut is a dry, hard, one-seeded fruit that does not split open when ripe (see BOTANY; FRUIT). Nuts have tough, woody outside walls, or shells. The nutmeat inside the shell is the seed and it is usually high in fat and protein. *Nut* can refer to just the nutmeat or the nutmeat and the shell. Some nuts, such as the chestnut, are mainly starch (see FAT; PROTEIN; SEED; STARCH).

Many nuts are grown as food crops. Almonds and peanuts are among the most important in world trade. Walnuts, filberts, pecans, hickory nuts, and macadamia nuts are the most common nut crops in the United States. As well as providing food, many nuts also provide valuable oils used in cooking, lubrication, wood finishing, and in the manufacture of cosmetics.

Many kinds of fruits and seeds that are popularly known as nuts are not true nuts. The peanut, for example, is actually a legume, or pod. Coconuts, walnuts, pecans, and hickory nuts are all drupes, but when we buy them, their outer fibrous or leatherlike coverings have been removed. Almonds are also drupes, but we often buy just the seeds, with the woody pit removed. Brazil nuts are seeds with very hard coats.

See also DRUPE; LEGUME.

NUTHATCH A nuthatch is a small bird that belongs to the family Sittidae. Its average length is 4.5 in. [11.5 cm]. The nuthatch was named for its habit of tucking nuts into cracks in the bark of trees to hold them in place while pecking them open. Besides nuts, seeds, and grain, the nuthatch eats mainly insects, which it searches for by creeping up and down trees. It is the only bird that can easily climb down a tree headfirst.

There are about twenty-five species of nuthatches in the world. Four species are found in North America. The best-known North American species is the white-breasted nuthatch. It has a gray back and wings; a short, gray tail; a long, slender bill; a black "cap" on top of its head; and a white breast. It lives in most parts of the United States and is commonly seen around bird feeders during the winter.

See also BIRD.

NUTHATCH

In winter, the nuthatch feeds by wedging a seed or nut into a gap in tree bark. It then hammers the seed open with blows from its powerful beak.

NUTRITION

Nutrition is the science of how the body uses food to provide energy, to support growth and repair of body tissues, and to maintain body functions. Nutrition deals with the digestion of food, the absorption and transportation of nutrients (nourishing substances contained in foods), and the metabolism of nutrients once they are transported to the individual cells of the body (see METABOLISM). Dietetics is an important branch of nutrition. Dietetics is concerned with people's food needs and the development of a balanced eating plan that meets these needs. Dietitians work in hospitals, schools, and other institutions.

Nutritionists work to define a diet that not only prevents disease but also promotes good health. To achieve their goal, nutritionists carry out research on how the nutrients function, the amount of each nutrient that people need, and the relationship between nutrients and disease. They have found that some diseases are the result of a lack of one or more nutrients, while other diseases seem to result from too much food (see DEFICIENCY DISEASES). However, nutrition is not an exact or fixed science. While new discoveries continue to add to nutritionists' understanding of how diet affects health, many aspects of nutrition are still not fully understood.

For example, even many years after the discovery of the nutrients called vitamins, their exact roles are not known (see VITAMIN). One such case involves vitamin D. Vitamin D cures and prevents rickets, a bone disease. Vitamin D is known to affect the absorption of the mineral calcium from the intestines. Calcium is a vital part of bone tissue. However, exactly how vitamin D performs its function is not clear.

Nutritionists do know that people need certain nutrients for building and maintaining healthy bodies. These nutrients are carbohydrates, fats, minerals, proteins, and vitamins. Water is also essential (see CARBOHYDRATE; FAT; MINERAL; PROTEIN; WATER).

There are three forms of carbohydrates—starch, sugar, and cellulose or fiber. A balanced intake of carbohydrates is needed for energy and regularity.

Fats are very concentrated energy sources. They make up part of the cell structure and protect vital organs. Foods that provide fat include butter, margarine, salad oils, nuts, eggs, meat, and such plant foods as corn, peanuts, and soybeans.

Minerals are needed by the body in small amounts. Calcium is largely responsible for the hardness of bones and teeth. Iodine, iron, magnesium, potassium, phosphorus, and zinc are among the other essential minerals.

Vitamins are essential to many body functions. They help release the energy from foods, promote normal growth, and keep the nerves and muscles functioning properly.

Protein builds the body's tissue and is a basic substance of every cell. It is found in foods of animal origin, such as meat (including fish and poultry), eggs, and milk. Protein is also found in some cereal grains, vegetables and fruits, legumes (such as soybeans and chickpeas), and nuts.

To encourage obtaining the right amounts of the nutrients, nutritionists stress the importance of varying one's food choices from day to day. They also warn against "empty calorie" foods, which provide a high proportion of calories to the amount of nutrients (see CALORIE).

HEALTHY DIET

A balanced diet includes a wide range of different kinds of foods, such as fruit and vegetables, nuts and other protein-rich foods, milk and dairy products, and grains, such as those used to make bread and pasta.

Malnutrition is a term used to refer to inadequate nourishment. People who experience malnutrition may develop certain diseases. In addition to rickets (mentioned above), diseases caused by lack of certain nutrients include kwashiorkor (protein deficiency), marasmus (protein-calorie deficiency), pellagra (niacin deficiency; niacin is a vitamin), and xerophthalmia (vitamin A deficiency).

In the past, malnutrition was the most important concern of nutritionists. In the United States today, however, obesity is a problem of equal or greater concern. Nutritionists estimate that over thirty million Americans are overweight. Obesity results from taking in more calories than the body needs. Excess calories are stored as fat. To lose weight, most nutritionists recommend the same advice they do for everyone: Eat a balanced diet. Overweight people should also reduce the number of calories eaten and exercise regularly. "Fad" diets or diets with extremely low calorie intakes can be harmful and usually do not have positive long-range results (see DIET).

MALNUTRITION

Malnutrition results from inadequate nourishment. The condition has recurred in parts of Africa in recent years when crops failed following drought. This malnourished child is in the Sudan.

Animal nutrition Most animals in the wild eat a balanced diet by instinct, but nutritional research is important in making sure that those in captivity, such as pets, farm animals, and animals in zoos, receive the right foods to stay healthy. Researchers have learned that different species of animals have distinct nutritional needs. For example, humans, guinea pigs, and monkeys require vitamin C to maintain health. However, many animals, such as rats, do not. Cats can eat meat without suffering from a buildup of cholesterol in the blood vessels the way humans do (see CHOLESTEROL). Scientists have developed special feeds for cattle, chickens, pigs, and other animals raised for food. These feeds contain exact amounts of nutrients needed by each animal. Vitamins, minerals, and other chemicals are often added to animals' feed, just as they are added to processed foods for humans (see FOOD PROCESSING).

The science of nutrition overlaps various other fields of science. Nutrition is part of medicine, physiology, and biochemistry (see BIOCHEMISTRY; MEDICINE; PHYSIOLOGY). Chemists make synthetic (human-made) foods from chemicals, and educators teach correct food habits. Researchers in agriculture also work to develop high-yield and high-quality crops.

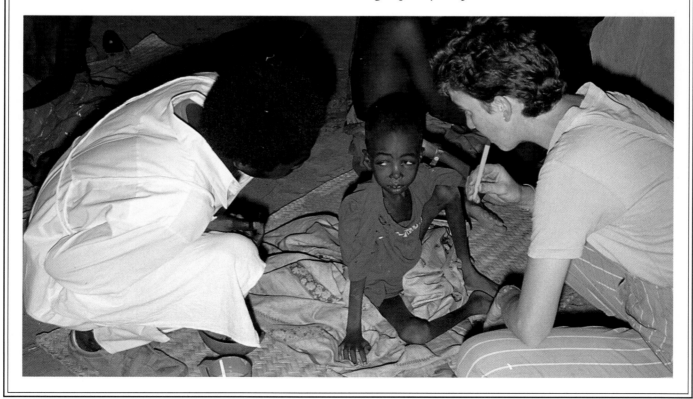

NYLON *Nylon* is the name for a family of synthetic (human-made) resins of the type known as thermoplastics. Thermoplastics are a group of plastics that become soft when heated and hard when cooled (see PLASTIC; RESIN). Nylon is one of the toughest, strongest, and most elastic substances known (see ELASTICITY). Nylon can be formed into fibers, bristles, sheets, rods, tubes, and coatings. It can also be made in powdered form for use in making molds. Nylon fabrics resist mildew and are not harmed by most kinds of oil, grease, and household cleaning fluids (see MILDEW). Nylon absorbs little water.

Most nylon (the first synthesized polymer) is made from two chemical compounds: hexamethylenediamine and adipic acid (see COMPOUND). Hexamethylenediamine contains carbon, hydrogen, and nitrogen. Adipic acid contains carbon, hydrogen, and oxygen. Manufacturers combine the two compounds to form a substance called nylon salt. A solution of nylon salt is placed in an autoclave (a heating device). The autoclave heats the solution under pressure. Water is removed, and the small molecules in the compound combine to form large molecules. This process is called polymerization (see POLYMERIZATION).

In some factories, the newly made nylon comes out of the machines as a plastic ribbon, which is then cooled and cut into small pieces. Nylon fibers are made by forcing molten (melted) nylon through tiny holes in a device called a spinneret. The thin streams of nylon that come out of the spinneret harden into threadlike filaments when they strike the air. Then, they are wound onto bobbins. From 1 to as many as 2,520 filaments are united into a nylon yarn used for clothing material. The fibers are stretched after they cool. This stretching action causes the molecules in the fibers to fall into a straight line, making the fibers stronger and more elastic.

Nylon was first made into hosiery in 1937. Since then, many uses have been found for it. Nylon is used to make carpets, clothing, fishing lines, parachutes, rope, and upholstery. Nylon is also used in tires and for bristles in many types of brushes. Solid pieces of nylon are used to make small machine parts, such as bearings and gears. Unlike metal machine parts, nylon machine parts need little lubrication.

E.I. du Pont de Nemours & Co., of the United States, was a leader in the development of nylon. Experimentation with it began in the 1920s, and Du Pont produced the first nylon in 1935. Called Nylon 66 because both chemicals used in making it have six carbon atoms, Nylon 66 is now produced by manufacturers around the world. There are several other forms of nylon manufactured today, including Nylon 6 and Qiana. Qiana is a silklike nylon fiber used in clothing.

See also FIBER; TEXTILE.

NYLON

Nylon is a useful plastic that can be used to make a wide variety of articles. Pictured here are fishing line, rope, gear wheels, a comb, brush bristles, and clothing.

NYMPH (nĭmf) A nymph is a stage in the growth of certain groups of insects. Most insects change in body shape and size several times before becoming an adult. These changes are called metamorphosis (see METAMORPHOSIS). The nymphal stage is part of the process known as incomplete metamorphosis. During the nymphal stage, young insects look similar to their parents although they have no fully developed wings. Nymphs shed their outer skins from time to time as they grow, in a process called molting (see MOLTING). Dragonflies, grasshoppers, termites, earwigs, and some other insects have a nymphal stage.

See also INSECT.

NYMPH

Dragonflies are among those insects that have several nymphal stages between the egg and adult. Dragonfly nymphs live in fresh water and feed on small aquatic creatures.

O

OAK Oaks are trees that belong to the beech family and to the genus *Quercus*. They can grow from 60 to 110 ft. [18 to 33.3 m] tall. The leaves of oaks usually have several lobes, or projections, along the edge. Many oaks are evergreens, but other species are deciduous. During the fall, the leaves of some of these trees turn brilliant colors. The fruit of the tree is called an acorn. An acorn is a small nut with a seed inside that is carried in a cuplike structure. Acorns are a source of food for wildlife (see BEECH FAMILY; LEAF; NUT; SEED).

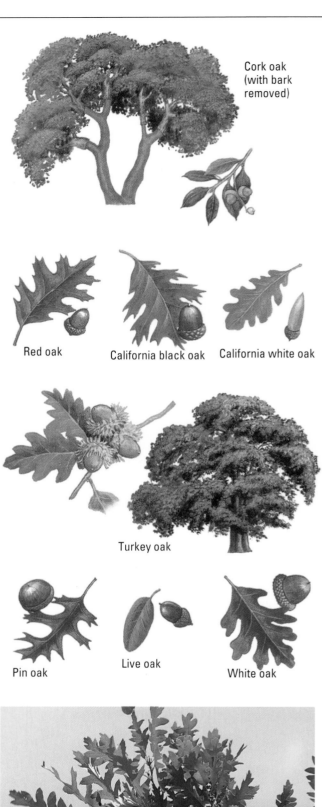

Cork oak (with bark removed)

Red oak

California black oak

California white oak

Turkey oak

Pin oak

Live oak

White oak

OAK

Many types of oak are pictured here. The photograph shows a fine-leaved variety called Turkey oak.

ACTIVITY *Find what lives in oaks*

As long as they are growing in their native areas, oak trees support huge numbers of insect species. You can get an idea of the number by spreading an old sheet under the branches and then shaking them vigorously. The insects will fall onto the sheet where you can see them easily. Plant bugs and earwigs are usually common, and there may be caterpillars and lacewings as well. There will also be many spiders. Try this project with different kinds of oak trees to see which have the most insect life. Also try it at different times of the year to see how the insects change with the seasons.

There are more than six hundred species of oak trees in the world. About half of those species grow in North America. Oaks grow naturally only in the Northern Hemisphere. They are a valuable source of wood for building and fuel.

OAK RIDGE NATIONAL LABORATORY

The Oak Ridge National Laboratory is where a great deal of nuclear technology has been developed. It is located in Oak Ridge, Tennessee, which is about 18 mi. [29 km] from Knoxville.

The Oak Ridge National Laboratory was founded in 1943 by the U.S. government as part of the Manhattan Project to develop the atomic bomb. Oak Ridge thrived during World War II (1939–1945), but it has now shrunk to about one-third of its peak size. Today, the Oak Ridge National Laboratory concerns itself with developing peaceful uses for nuclear energy. Other research includes radioactive drugs and the conversion of salt water into fresh water.

See also DESALINATION; NUCLEAR ENERGY; NUCLEAR WEAPONS; RADIOACTIVITY.

OATS Oats are important cereal crops that can grow in poor-quality soil. They can also grow in cooler and wetter regions than most other cereals. They are members of the genus *Avena* of the grass family. Oats are related to corn, barley, wheat, and rice. The oat plant reaches a height of about 3.3 ft. [1 m]. It has forty to fifty side branches, each of which ends in a flower cluster called a spikelet. Each spikelet contains two seeds that are enclosed in husks (see CEREAL CROP; FLOWER; GRASS; SEED).

Oats have the highest food value of any of the cereal crops. Oats are rich in carbohydrates, proteins, fats, calcium, iron, and vitamin B_1. Oats are grown mainly to feed livestock. The seeds, once removed from the husks, also can be used to make oatmeal, breakfast cereals, cakes, and cookies. Adding the outer coat of the seeds, called the bran, to various foods became very popular in the late 1980s. Some studies showed that eating oat bran helped lower cholesterol levels in humans. High levels of cholesterol in the blood are believed to contribute to heart disease (see CHOLESTEROL; HEART DISEASE). However, other studies have suggested that oat bran may not reduce cholesterol any more than do other foods that contain fiber, such as other cereals, dried peas and beans, vegetables, and fruits.

OATS

Oats are rich in nutrients and have the highest food value of any of the cereal crops.

OBSERVATORY An observatory is usually a building that is designed for the study of the galaxies, planets, stars, and other parts of the universe. Astronomers study the universe at observatories using telescopes (see ASTRONOMY; TELESCOPE).

People of ancient civilizations, such as those of Babylonia, Greece, and Egypt, were the first to study the movements and changes in the appearance of the moon, planets, and stars, including the sun. The invention of telescopes at the start of the seventeenth century A.D. marked the single most important advance in astronomical observation. Before that time, astronomers used instruments that included the astrolabe, sextant, and quadrant (see ASTROLABE; NAVIGATION; QUADRANT). By 1610, the Italian scientist Galileo had made many discoveries using a simple telescope (see GALILEO). Today's precise equipment, such as the photometer, spectroscope, and even the computer, have important uses for astronomers (see PHOTOMETRY; SPECTROSCOPE).

OBSERVATORY

Earth-bound observatories are usually built on a hill or mountain, where the air is clear. Pictured above is the McDonald Observatory in Fort Davis in West Texas.

Modern observatories have telescopes called optical telescopes that use lenses, mirrors, and cameras to record the visible light that is being sent from bodies in space. Other telescopes called radio telescopes are also used. Radio telescopes detect radio waves coming from outer space (see RADIO ASTRONOMY).

Observatories with optical telescopes are usually located at high altitudes and away from large cities. This minimizes any blurring effects that the atmosphere might have on light waves from space. City lights and pollution also cause problems for astronomers. The rapid growth of cities has made finding appropriate sites difficult.

Since the 1960s, various countries have sent observatories with telescopes and other equipment into space. These telescopes can view space and detect light and other radiations without any interference from the earth's atmosphere. The largest reflecting space telescope, called the Hubble Space Telescope (HST), was launched into orbit around Earth in 1990. Because of an error in the way one of the mirrors of the HST was manufactured, some of the first images sent back to Earth were distorted. Astronauts repaired the telescope in 1993, resulting in dramatically sharper images.
See also UNIVERSE.

OBSIDIAN (ŏb sĭd′ ē ən) Obsidian is volcanic glass. It forms when molten (melted) lava cools too quickly for crystals to form. It is usually black and sometimes has red streaks. The chemical composition of obsidian is the same as that of granite. Obsidian breaks easily into sharp fragments. These fragments were once used by native Americans for arrowheads. Obsidian is also used in jewelry and other art objects.
See also CRYSTAL; GRANITE; LAVA; VOLCANO.

OBSIDIAN

Obsidian is a brittle, glassy mineral that forms when volcanic lava cools slowly.

An ocean is a large body of salt water. There are smaller bodies of salt water called bays, gulfs, seas, and sounds. There are four oceans: the Atlantic, Pacific, Indian, and Arctic. All of these bodies of water are connected to each other.

Ocean currents The water in the oceans is not still, but instead moves in regular patterns. These patterns are made up of currents. Currents are strong movements of water in one direction. There are many kinds of currents. One kind is a stream. A stream is a current with distinct boundaries. The Gulf Stream, off the east coast of North America, is an example of a stream. It flows from near the Gulf of Mexico north to Canada. The Gulf Stream is almost like a river in the middle of the Atlantic Ocean. A drift is a current that does not have distinct boundaries. In a drift, the water in one area of the ocean shifts slowly in a general direction.

Currents are caused by several things. Winds push water into currents. Differences in water temperature and salt content in different parts of the oceans cause currents, too. Cold and salty water is denser than warm and less salty water. When cold, salty water sinks, it pushes other water up, causing currents. Currents are also caused by the rotation (spin) of the earth. The circulation of seawater in the Northern Hemisphere is clockwise, while the circulation in the Southern Hemisphere is counterclockwise (see HEMISPHERE).

Tides are a type of regular current, changing direction every six hours. They are caused mostly by the gravitational pull of the moon (see GRAVITY; TIDE).

Currents are important to the plants and animals in the oceans. The movement of water helps bring them food. It also helps them during migrations (see MIGRATION). Currents also affect the climate of land (see CLIMATE). In the past, currents helped sailors move from one land to another, leading to widespread exploration of the earth.

Ocean waves Waves are temporary movements of water for short distances. They are usually caused by winds. Some waves can be caused by something moving through the water, such as a ship, or a movement underwater, such as an earthquake. Waves usually affect only the surface water. They are rarely higher than 3.2 ft. [1 m] but may reach 40 ft. [12 m] in height during storms. The largest wave recorded, which was caused by an earthquake, was 112 ft. [34 m] high. Waves caused by earthquakes or by hurricanes far out in the ocean are erroneously called tidal waves. They are really tsunamis (see HURRICANE; TSUNAMI; WAVE).

Ocean floor The bottom of the ocean is called the floor. It is also called the ocean bed. The ocean floor is similar to the land near the water. It has flat areas, valleys, and mountain ranges. Islands are the tops of underwater mountains that stick out of the water. Some of these mountains are volcanoes (see VOLCANO).

The ocean is shallowest near land. Land gradually slopes under water. This slope is called the continental shelf (see CONTINENTAL SHELF). Much sea life and valuable resources, such as oil, are found in the continental shelf. The continental shelf slopes gently to the continental edge. There, the steep continental slope begins and extends to deep areas of the ocean called the abyssal zone. There are deep valleys, or trenches, at the bottom of the abyssal zone (see ABYSSAL ZONE). The Mariana Trench in the Pacific Ocean is the deepest point in the world. There, the ocean floor is 35,275 ft. [10,752 m] deep. That translates to over 6 mi. [10 km] deep.

The cooperative work of scientists who took part in the International Geophysical Year of 1957–1958 set the stage for great advances in oceanography. The discovery of the Mid-Atlantic Ridge—a huge underwater mountain range in the Atlantic Ocean—and the record-breaking dive into the Mariana Trench by the U.S. Navy's bathyscaphe *Trieste* early in 1960 were only the beginning (see BATHYSPHERE AND BATHYSCAPHE). Oceanographic institutions all over the world quickly started large-scale projects to expand and apply the new knowledge. They also applied advanced technology, borrowing the best that electronics and modern engineering could offer.

A notable example was the Deep Sea Drilling Project of the National Science Foundation (NSF), which lasted from 1966 to 1983. This program used a converted offshore oil rig vessel, the *Glomar Challenger,* to drill and bring up samples of sediment,

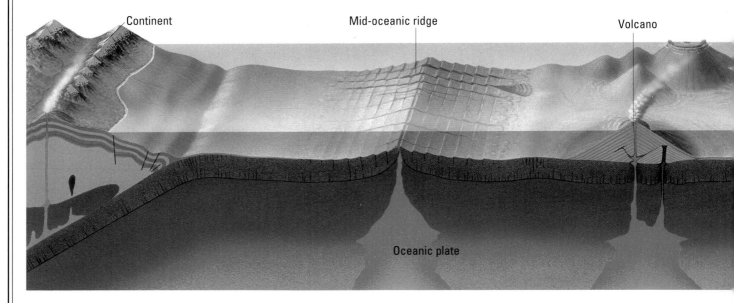

Continent · Mid-oceanic ridge · Volcano

Oceanic plate

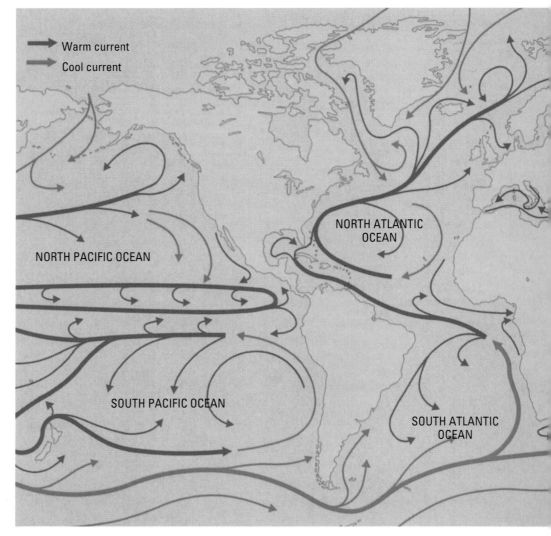

Warm current
Cool current

NORTH ATLANTIC OCEAN

NORTH PACIFIC OCEAN

SOUTH PACIFIC OCEAN

SOUTH ATLANTIC OCEAN

OCEAN CURRENTS
This map (right) shows the world's major ocean currents. They tend to circulate in the major oceans, bringing cool water from polar seas toward the equatorial region.

called cores, from the ocean floor. These cores provided additional evidence to support the theory of continental drift (see CONTINENTAL DRIFT; OIL RIG; SEDIMENTARY ROCK). In 1984, the NSF began a new project called the Ocean Drilling Program using a more advanced ship, the *JOIDES Resolution.* This ship made its first cruise in 1985. On board the drilling ship is some of the most

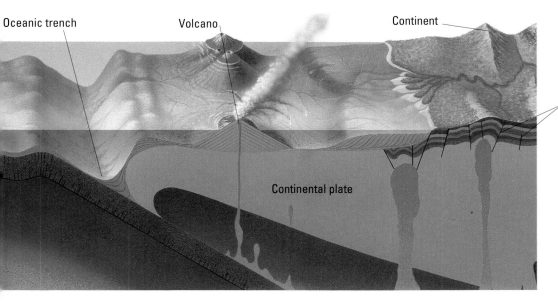

Oceanic trench   Volcano   Continent

Fault lines

Continental plate

OCEAN FLOOR

The ocean floor is the upper part of the oceanic crust, which is formed along mid-oceanic ridges by molten rock that wells up from the earth's mantle (left). An oceanic plate may collide with a continental plate, forming an oceanic trench where the oceanic plate is forced downward.

advanced oceanographic research equipment in the world. The ship also has two mainframe computers that are linked to fifty small computers located throughout the ship (see COMPUTER).

One of the great modern aids to ocean research has been the development of small submarines (see SUBMARINE). One such vessel is the Woods Hole (Massachusetts) Oceanographic Institution's *Alvin. Alvin*'s 1977 exploration of the Galápagos Rift Valley in the Pacific Ocean startled the world. Looking for a cause of previously observed high temperatures in waters more than 8,000 ft. [2,500 m] deep, the *Alvin* crew discovered vents that poured hot water into the icy ocean from beneath its floor. Some of the vents were almost 30 ft. [9 m] high. Water at temperatures of up to 570°F [300°C] poured from the vents. Minerals, such as cadmium, copper, and nickel, were dissolved in the water. This discovery provided new insights into how mineral deposits form.

Marine biologists later discovered that previously unknown forms of sea life were living around the vents. They found that giant shellfish and tube worms up to 9 ft. [3 m] long are able to live at these depths without sunlight. They obtain the energy they need from bacteria that thrive in the hot water.

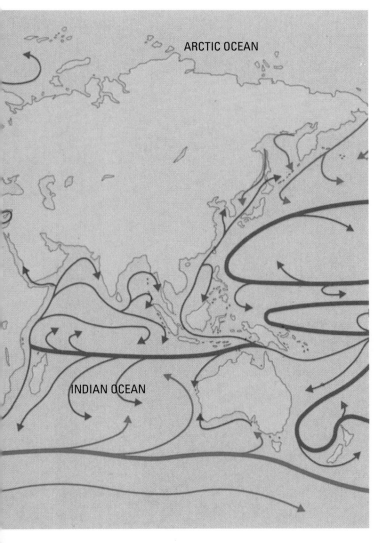

ARCTIC OCEAN

INDIAN OCEAN

OCEANOGRAPHY (ō´ shə nŏg´ rə fē)

Oceanography is the study of the oceans of the world (see OCEAN). Although oceans cover 71 percent of the earth's surface, relatively little is known about them. Oceanography is one of the youngest sciences.

Oceanography is divided into four branches. Physical oceanography is the study of the temperature, currents, tides, and ice formation of the oceans. Geological oceanography is the study of the coastlines, islands, and floor of the oceans. Chemical oceanography is the study of the chemicals in seawater. Biological oceanography is the study of the living organisms in the oceans.

OCEANOGRAPHY

Oceanographers (scientists who study oceans) often work from ships at sea. The oceanographers pictured are studying the Black Sea. They collect samples of the water to study such things as temperature and salt content. They also capture sea creatures and take samples of material from the seafloor.

It is usually called marine biology (see MARINE BIOLOGY).

OCELOT (ŏs´ ə lŏt´)

The ocelot is a cat found from southern Arizona and Texas in the United States to Paraguay and northern Argentina in South America.

The ocelot lives in forests, spending most of its life on the ground. However, the ocelot can also climb well. It often hunts in trees.

The ocelot is considered a medium-sized cat. Including its tail, it is about 3.5 to 4.5 ft. [107 to 120 cm] long.

Ocelots are nocturnal hunters. They feed on birds, mice, monkeys, rabbits, and snakes.

The coat of the ocelot varies greatly in color, from reddish yellow to gray, and has black spots. The belly is usually white, marked with black.

Two kittens are normally produced in a

OCELOT

The ocelot is a rare medium-sized wild cat that is found in forests and woods from southwestern North America to central South America. It is a nocturnal hunter that feeds on small animals.

litter. The animals have been hunted nearly to extinction for their fur.

See also CAT; EXTINCTION; NOCTURNAL BEHAVIOR.

OCTANE RATING (ŏk′ tān′ rāt′ ĭng) Octane rating is a way of describing the quality of gasoline. The higher the octane number, the less likely a gasoline will produce a noise called "knocking" in an internal combustion engine. Internal combustion engines are engines used in automobiles, motorcycles, and trucks. In an internal combustion engine, the fuel is mixed with air and burned. The burning should take place smoothly. Knocking occurs when the fuel burns too soon or too quickly and explodes. Knocking weakens the engine and causes it to lose power (see ENGINE; GASOLINE).

Gasoline manufacturers determine the octane rating of gasolines using a test-fuel mixture of two hydrocarbons: isooctane and normal heptane (see HYDROCARBON). Isooctane causes hardly any knocking and is given an octane rating of one hundred. Normal heptane causes severe knocking and is given an octane rating of zero. Gasolines are compared with test-fuel mixtures and then given their ratings. For example, a gasoline might have an octane rating of 98. This means it knocks as much as a mixture of 98 percent isooctane and 2 per cent normal heptane.

OCTOPUS The octopus is a marine mollusk belonging to the class Cephalopoda (see CEPHALO-POD; MOLLUSCA). There are about 150 species of octopuses. They live in seas all over the world but are most common in the warmer seas. Some swim in the surface layers, but most live on the seabed, usually close to the coasts. The octopus has no outside shell. Its eight sucker-covered arms (called tentacles) spread out from a soft, baglike body. Most octopuses are only a little bigger than a person's fist. However, the largest ones may measure 28 ft. [8.5 m] from the tip of one tentacle to the tip of another on the opposite side of the body.

The octopus has large, shiny eyes and strong, hard jaws. The latter can deliver a poisonous bite. Most octopuses feed on crabs, lobsters, and other crustaceans (see CRUSTACEAN). These animals are caught by the octopus's tentacles, and their shells are easily cracked by the octopus's jaws. If an octopus loses a tentacle, a new one grows in its place in a process called regeneration (see REGENERA-TION). The octopus has the most highly developed brain of all the invertebrates (animals without

OCTOPUS
The octopus has no outside shell. It has eight sucker-covered tentacles, or arms, which spread out from its soft body. Most octopuses live in warm waters.

backbones). When disturbed, the octopus darts away, squirting out a black fluid. This fluid forms a dark cloud to confuse the attacker and hide the octopus. Also, when an octopus becomes excited, it changes color, becoming brown, gray, red, purple, blue, white, and sometimes even striped. Some octopuses can change color to blend in with their surroundings.
See also CAMOUFLAGE.

OHM (ōm) The ohm is the unit of electrical resistance. The electrical resistance in ohms can be calculated by dividing the voltage applied to a substance by the current that passes through it. The current is measured in units called amperes. For example, if six volts results in a current of three amperes, the substance has a resistance of two ohms. The ohm is named after the German scientist Georg Ohm. The symbol for the ohm is the Greek letter Ω. It is called omega.
See also AMPERE; CURRENT, ELECTRIC; OHM, GEORG SIMON; RESISTANCE, ELECTRICAL; VOLT.

OHM, GEORG SIMON (1787–1854) (ōm, gā ôrk′ zē′ mōn) Georg Ohm was a German physicist. He made important discoveries in the study of electricity. His most famous discovery is now called Ohm's law. Ohm's law shows that the size of the

current in a substance depends on its resistance and the voltage. The unit of resistance, the ohm, is named after him. Ohm also studied sound. He helped found the science of acoustics.
See also ACOUSTICS; ELECTRICITY; OHM; OHM'S LAW.

OHM'S LAW Ohm's law (ōm′z lô) is a very important law in electricity. Ohm's law states that the size of the current passing through a substance depends on two things—the size of the voltage applied to the substance and the electrical resistance of the substance (see CURRENT, ELECTRIC; ELECTRICITY; RESISTANCE, ELECTRICAL; VOLT). This law is written as:

$$I = V/R.$$

I is the current measured in amperes (see AMPERE). *V* is the voltage. *R* is the resistance measured in ohms (see OHM). The current increases as the voltage increases. However, the current decreases as the resistance increases. The law is only accurate for substances that are good conductors of electricity, such as metals (see CONDUCTION OF ELECTRICITY). Also, the temperature has to remain the same for the law to hold, because resistance varies with temperature. Thus, Ohm's law is never completely accurate because a current heats up a substance in which it flows. This increased temperature causes the resistance to increase. The law is named after the German scientist Georg Ohm.
See also OHM, GEORG SIMON.